COMPLETE
SAILING MANUAL

NH
NEW
HOLLAND

COMPLETE
SAILING MANUAL

Jeff Toghill

First published in 2005 by New Holland Publishers
London • Cape Town • Sydney • Auckland
www.newhollandpublishers.com

Garfield House
86 Edgware Rd
London W2 2EA
United Kingdom

80 McKenzie St
Cape Town
8001
South Africa

14 Aquatic Drive
Frenchs Forest
NSW 2086
Australia

218 Lake Rd
Northcote
Auckland
New Zealand

Publisher Mariëlle Renssen
Publishing managers Claudia dos Santos (SA),
Simon Pooley (UK)
Commissioning editor Alfred LeMaitre
Editor Gill Gordon
Consultant Simon Jinks (RYA Yachtmaster
Instructor Examiner)

Senior designer Richard MacArthur
Designer Robert Last
Illustrators Robert Last, Stephen Felmore
Picture research Karla Kik, Tamlyn McGeean
Production Myrna Collins
Proofreader Anna Tanneberger

ISBN 1 84330 881 9

Reproduction by Resolution Colour (Pty) Ltd., Cape Town
Printed and bound in Malaysia by Times Offset (M). Sdn. Bhd.

1 3 5 7 9 10 8 6 4 2

*Keelboat sailing is about the thrill of the open air, feeling the wind in your hair and the tang of saltwater on your skin. Whether your
ambitions are to race competitively or simply to have fun, once hooked, you'll be addicted for life.*

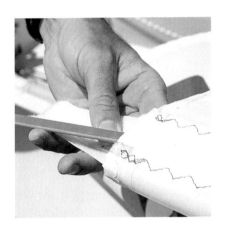

CONTENTS

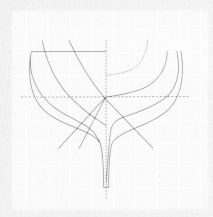 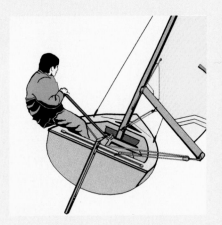 

HOW A BOAT SAILS

Many people are mystified by the way in which a boat floats. If you throw a piece of steel into the ocean it will immediately sink, yet big ships, which are made of thousands of tonnes of steel, float quite happily on the same ocean. The answer to this puzzling phenomenon was first discovered by the Greek mathematician Archimedes. While sitting in his bath he realized that, when he filled it to the brim, the water overflowed when he climbed into it, indicating that his body was displacing some of the water.

Taking it further, Archimedes discovered that when his body floated, the amount of water displaced was exactly the same weight as his body. This led him to the theory that when an object is immersed in water, an upward force, called buoyancy, is exerted upon it. When this upward force (the weight of the water displaced) equals the downwards pressure (the weight of the object), the body floats.

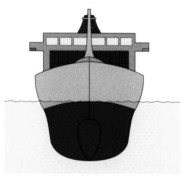 

A yacht sails best when it has the correct buoyancy (top centre); if it is too high or too low in the water, it won't achieve the same efficiency of speed and performance. The same principle applies when cargo is loaded into a freighter, causing it to sink lower in the water.

Buoyancy

Because the hull of a big ship has a huge volume and can therefore displace an enormous amount of water, it floats. On the other hand, a small piece of steel displaces very little water so there is virtually no buoyancy to hold it up and it sinks. This basic explanation of how a boat floats can be illustrated by the way in which a freighter with no cargo in its hull floats high in the water but sinks deeper as cargo is loaded (see illustration above). The hull shape remains the same, so the upward force of buoyancy stays the same, but the weight of the cargo increases the downward pressure, making the boat settle lower in the water.

If cargo was continuously added, there would come a point where the ship would disappear under the water but, before that happens the ship reaches the point which has been determined by the builders as the optimum flotation position. At that point, the ship is stabilized, with its total weight equal to the weight of the displaced water.

The same applies to yachts, which are designed to float at a level that will give maximum speed and performance, according to the shape of the hull, combined with the purpose of the boat. A lightweight, fast racing yacht is more buoyant than a heavy cruiser.

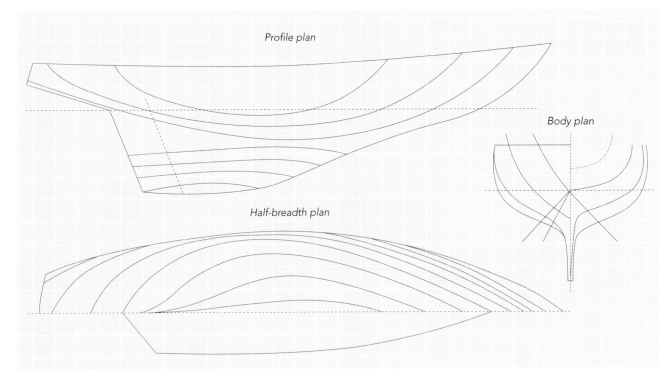

Profile plan

Body plan

Half-breadth plan

The shape of the hull has a direct bearing on a boat's speed through the water. The more streamlined the shape, the faster the yacht.

Hull shape

While weight is an important factor in governing the way a boat floats, the designer must take the whole underwater area of the hull into consideration when deciding how the boat will perform. The shape and size of this area determine how fast the boat will go, how sea-worthy it will be in a seaway and what sort of internal accommoda-tion it will provide.

Weight also impacts on a boat's stability, as the type and shape of the keel, and the amount of ballast fitted to it, determine how stable the boat is. A deep keel with heavy ballast provides maximum stability, while a retractable centreboard keel, leeboard or bilge keel add less stability to the hull.

Hull shape and weight are some of the factors a naval architect must bear in mind when designing a boat, taking account of the type of vessel it is intended to be.

The design of a small centre-board dinghy will, of course, be fairly basic, but modern hi tech ocean-racing yachts are built from very complex plans.

Apart from a sail plan, rigging plan and a general layout plan (for the interior accommodation), the hull lines are usually drawn up in the form of three main plans: a profile plan, half-breadth plan and a body plan, which together show the shape of the boat's hull from all angles and enable the builder to construct the yacht exactly to the designer's specifications.

The profile plan shows the yacht's hull as seen from the starboard side (see p189), with contour lines (known as bow and buttock lines) indicating the shape of the hull, just as contour lines on a map show the shape of hills and valleys; the lines for the port side (see p189) are, of course, identical.

The half-breadth plan is similar to the profile plan but this time looking upwards from beneath the keel. In order to save space, only half the boat is drawn on this plan, hence the name, and the outside contour is the deck line.

The body plan shows the cross-section shape of the hull from the bow to the midships section on one side and from the stern to the midships section on the other.

Stability

One of the most important features in the design of a sailing boat is its stability. When you step into a small dinghy, it will tilt towards the side on which you stand, as a result of your weight moving the centre of gravity across the boat.

The upward force of buoyancy acts on the centre of the boat, through a point known as the centre of buoyancy (B) while the weight of the boat acts downward through the centre of gravity (G). When point G is directly above point B the boat is stable and will not tip over. When the boat tilts (heels) as you step aboard, B and G are no longer in the same line.

The centre of buoyancy moves to the right or left of the centre of gravity as the boat tilts in that direction. However, because buoyancy pushes upwards and gravity pushes downwards, together they create a turning lever which will attempt to bring the boat back into the upright position.

This is known as the righting moment or righting lever – the force which counteracts the heel and gives the boat stability.

A good example of this can be seen when the boat is sailing. The pressure of the wind on the sails heels the boat and moves B to one side of G, so the natural tendency is for B and G to create a righting lever to bring the boat back to the upright; the actions of a stable boat.

However, there is a limit to the righting lever and, when the downward action of G gets to the other side of the upward action of B, the righting moment is reversed, and it becomes a turning moment, causing the boat to capsize as the boat has lost its initial stability. To prevent a capsize, the stability factors must be returned to where they were when the boat was upright, with G directly over B. There are two ways of doing this:

1. Reducing pressure in the sails by spilling wind. This enables the boat to return to the upright position and bring G back over B. It is usually done by slacking or easing the sheets (see p189).

2. Using crew weight or ballast to increase the righting lever and counter the heel. In dinghies, the crew act as ballast, leaning out on the high side of the boat (or in a trapeze) to pull the boat back to the upright. On a keel yacht the weight of the ballast keel is used. As the hull heels, the keel is lifted to one side, creating a strong righting moment that pulls the yacht back to the upright.

B – centre of buoyancy
G – centre of gravity

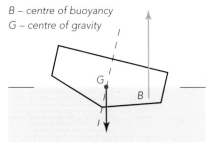
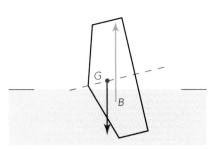

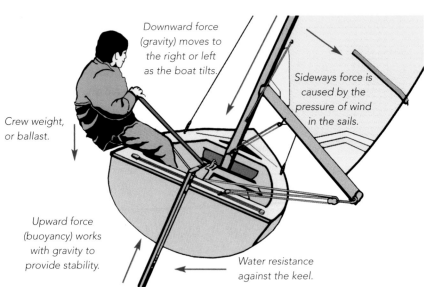

Downward force (gravity) moves to the right or left as the boat tilts.

Sideways force is caused by the pressure of wind in the sails.

Crew weight, or ballast.

Upward force (buoyancy) works with gravity to provide stability.

Water resistance against the keel.

Several forces act simultaneously to create a stable boat, notably the sideways force of the wind in the sail, countered by the force of water against the keel. In a centreboard dinghy (as above), the crew's weight helps to counter heel; in keel boats, ballast is used.

In theory, the ideal is for the boat to be sailed upright. This does not work in practice, because the pressure of wind in the sails causes the boat to heel and, without pressure in the sails, a boat will not move. So a compromise is reached where the two techniques described above are adapted to enable the boat to heel safely to the point where it is performing at its maximum, yet neither compromising safety nor risking a capsize.

The skill of the skipper and crew in balancing buoyancy and gravity determines how well the boat performs in any circumstances. (The sailing techniques used to achieve this are described in chapter 3.)

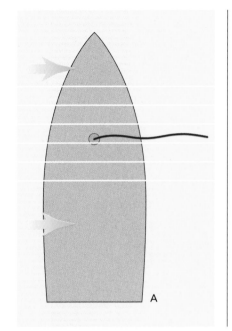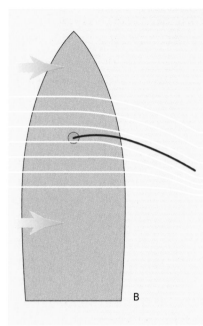

This diagram shows how sails offer little resistance to the wind (A), until sheeted on (B), which disrupts the air flow and creates a motive force.

Sail shape

It is not hard to understand how a boat sails with the wind coming from behind; pressure caused by wind on the sail simply pushes the boat forward. However, it is a totally different matter when the wind is ahead because the tendency will be for the boat to go backwards rather than forwards. Yet sailboats can and do sail into the wind – albeit not directly into it! It is often hard for the uninitiated to understand how a boat can sail close to the wind from which it is deriving its power.

The secret lies in the shape of the sails. In the days when windjammers roamed the oceans they had mostly square sails with little shape, which just gathered wind to push them along and, as a result,

they found it difficult to sail into the wind. Indeed, the trade routes they followed around the world were planned so that they had the wind behind them, or nearly behind them, most of the time.

Many a fine clipper deliberately made large detours across the oceans just to pick up a favourable following wind. One of the major sailing ship routes in the southern hemisphere ran from the Cape of Good Hope across the Southern Ocean to Australia and thence on to the infamous Cape Horn in South America. Ships sailed constantly eastwards on this track in order to use the favourable westerly winds that exist in the deep southern latitudes, often making speeds of 16 or 17 knots on a passage, even with their inefficient

square sails. It would have been almost impossible for them to sail in the opposite direction.

The invention of the fore and aft sail, which enabled a vessel to make progress into the wind, revolutionized sailing. While it is still not possible to sail directly into the wind, this type of sail enables high performance yachts to sail at a very close angle into the wind and thus make good progress in an upwind direction.

By sailing with the wind at a close angle, first on one side of the boat and then the other, a boat can reach a destination that is directly into the wind – a technique known as 'tacking' or 'beating' (see p47).

Just how close to the wind each boat can sail depends mainly on its design and the cut of its sails.

The sail maker's skill is judged to a great degree by the acuteness of this angle; a factor known as 'pointing'. Cruising yachts with average-cut sails may point to within 45 degrees of the wind, while high-performance yachts, like the huge sloops of the America's Cup races, with their expertly cut (and very expensive) sails, can sail at a much finer angle.

To understand how a sail derives power from the wind and drives the boat forward, we must first look at the shape of the sail and the way in which the air flows around it. Most fore and aft sails are cut and sewn into a shape not unlike the aerofoil section of an aircraft wing and, indeed, a sail works on much the same principle as a wing. The main difference is that while an aircraft wing is mounted horizontally and gains upward lift from the airflow around it, a sail is mounted vertically and gains forward drive from the airflow.

If sails had no shape, but were flat and evenly bisected the airflow, there would be no forward drive because the air would flow equally on either side. But, because sails have an aerofoil shape, air travelling around the outside of the curve travels faster than air on the inside of the curve. The faster airflow on the outside of the curve creates a vortex effect which tends to 'suck' the curve towards it. In the case of an aircraft wing, this suction pulls the wing (and therefore the

aircraft) upwards. In the case of a yacht, it pulls the sail (and thus the boat) forwards.

(To help understand this, picture a line of soldiers wheeling around a corner. On the inside of the curve, the innermost soldier marks time in one position, hardly moving, while the soldier on the outside almost has to run to keep up.)

To speed up the airflow on the outside of the curve and increase the vortex effect, an overlapping sail is mostly used to create a 'slot effect' between the sails. This is the most common rig for modern sailboats, with the foresail or jib overlapped around the mainsail to form the slot (see p33).

Because sails have an aerofoil shape, air travelling around the outside of the curve travels faster than the air inside the curve, creating a vortex which pulls the boat forward.

Centre of Effort

Wind exerts pressure right across the surface of a sail but, for the purposes of calculation, a theoretical point is adopted roughly in the centre. This is found by bisecting the angles at the three corners of the sail. Where these lines meet is the point through which the wind forces are said to be acting – the Centre of Effort. The result of pressure in the sails creates a twofold motion – forwards and sideways. The forward motion is required but the sideways motion is not, and some means of converting it to forward movement is necessary.

Centre of Lateral Resistance

Some centreboard dinghies, such as the Laser or Moth, are effectively flat bottomed and the pressure of wind through the Centre of Effort of the sail would send them skimming sideways across the surface of the water. To counteract this, a centreboard is lowered vertically beneath the hull to create resistance to the sideways movement.

Larger yachts have a permanent structure, in the form of one or more keels, which projects downwards under the hull to counteract the sideways drift. Like a sail, the keel (or centreboard) has a theoretical point through which the counteracting pressure is said to work. This point is called the Centre of Lateral Resistance. With the wind pushing the boat sideways through the

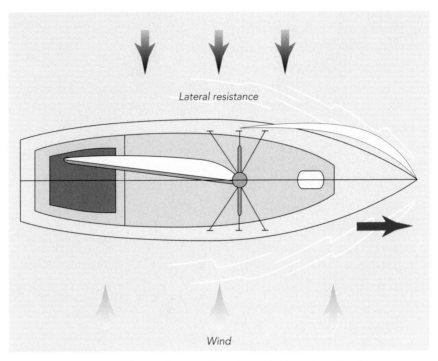

Together, the pressure, or force, of wind in the sails and the force (lateral resistance) provided by water against the keel, create forward movement.

Centre of Effort, and the water counteracting through the Centre of Lateral Resistance, a situation arises where the boat is squeezed between two pincer forces, rather like an orange pip squeezed between forefinger and thumb. Like the pip, the boat shoots forward, transferring all the related forces into forward movement (see diagram above). This simple explanation provides a basic illustration of what makes a boat sail into or across the wind.

Of course, when sailing with the wind coming from behind, there is no sideways drift and the wind just pushes the boat forwards. (This is why the centreboard is usually retracted when a dinghy is running before the wind.)

The wetted surface

The part of the hull above the waterline is referred to as the 'topsides' or 'freeboard' and the area below the waterline is termed the 'wetted surface'. Although the keel is the dominant factor, other parts of the wetted surface affect a boat's performance. For this reason, the designer will use every advantage he can to improve the forward drive and performance of the boat, by adjusting the shape of the hull beneath the waterline.

As a result, different sailboats vary considerably in their underwater shape and construction. Some have a 'fine entry' at the bow, enabling the hull to slip easily through the water, others favour a bluff bow because it permits more

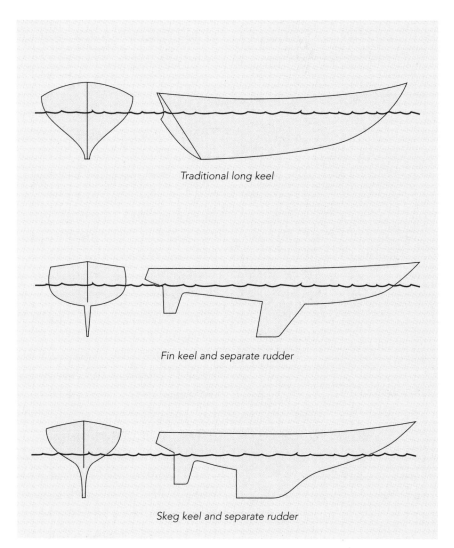

Traditional long keel

Fin keel and separate rudder

Skeg keel and separate rudder

Keel shape and hull type vary according to the purpose of the boat. Some sturdy cruisers have a broad hull with a long, deep keel (top) for good stability, while sleek racing yachts (bottom) have a narrow hull, enabling them to glide through the water.

interior room. Rudders vary in shape and design according to the intended use of the boat, and some yachts even have twin rudders.

But undoubtedly, the main underwater factor affecting a boat's performance is the type of keel fitted. There are fin keels, long keels, deep keels, retractable keels, bilge keels, even leeboards; all intended to create maximum lateral resistance while keeping water friction to a minimum.

High-powered racing yachts usually have thin, narrow keels that enable them to speed through the water and pivot quickly, like a top spinning on its axis. Ocean-going cruising boats require a more 'sea-kindly' keel to ride over big waves at sea. This type of keel is deep and long, often running for some length under the boat, giving it good steering stability when running down the face of big waves.

Because centreboard dinghies do not encounter big seas, but spend their time racing around harbours and estuaries, they have thin fin keels like racing yachts, but with the added advantage that they are retractable and can be adjusted for different points of sailing or for running up on a beach.

The lateral resistance of a keel or centreboard is at its maximum when vertically underneath the boat, i.e. when the boat is upright and the keel at its deepest.

As the boat heels to the wind, the effect of the keel is reduced, both by the fact that it is lifted from its deepest position and because the surface of the keel is angled, thus offering less lateral resistance to the water.

A similar situation arises with the sails, for they too lose efficiency as the boat heels; the wind starts to 'bleed' over the top, which means they lose power and effectiveness.

Theoretically, a boat should perform at its best when in the upright position but, in practice, some degree of heel cannot be avoided if the boat is to gain power from the wind. Finding what angle gives maximum performance on each individual boat is the secret of successful sailing, especially racing. It can be found only by experience with each individual boat and the suit of sails it carries.

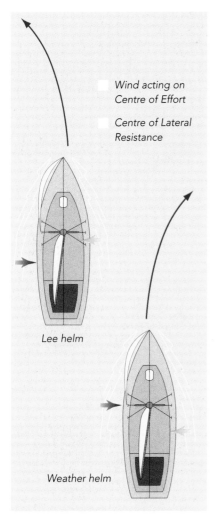

Wind acting on
Centre of Effort

Centre of Lateral
Resistance

Lee helm

Weather helm

Balance results from the interplay between the Centre of Effort and the Centre of Lateral Resistance.

Balancing and tuning the boat

In the fore and aft line of the boat, the Centre of Effort and the Centre of Lateral Resistance are never located directly above one another and are therefore never in balance.

If the Centre of Effort is astern of the Centre of Lateral Resistance, the boat will constantly try to turn into the wind, needing correction with the rudder, a condition known as 'weather helm'. If the reverse applies, and the Centre of Effort is ahead of the Centre of Lateral Resistance, the boat's head (bow) will constantly fall away from the wind, requiring rudder adjustment known as 'lee helm'.

Apart from the frustration of constantly adjusting the helm to counter these conditions, any use of the rudder acts like a brake on the boat's forward motion, so it is important to balance the two factors so that the boat sails straight ahead. However, this is difficult to achieve, for the interplay of sails and keel changes all the time. A boat which is balanced nicely in light winds may be hard to handle in stronger gusts due to the different sails used for stronger winds and the different wetted surface as the boat heels hard over.

To achieve the best balance for existing conditions, the boat must be 'tuned', a complex task involving adjustment to sails, rigging and other parts of the boat. The aim of tuning is to get the boat to move straight forward with minimum of rudder movements while extracting maximum power from the wind. This requires experience and skill on the part of the skipper, the sail maker and the rigger.

As tuning is a complex procedure, only the basics can be dealt with here. While the main requirements are fairly standard, the skill of fine-tuning individual yachts is acquired through experience, much of it gained on the particular vessel being tuned. For example, a sail maker preparing to cut a wardrobe of sails for a new ocean-going yacht will make at least three suits; for heavy weather, moderate weather and light winds. Each suit will be cut from different cloths; as lightweight sails will blow out in strong winds, whereas sails cut from heavy cloth will not set properly in light breezes.

Apart from the sails, there are other factors involved in tuning, such as setting up the rigging. Once again, this varies from boat to boat according to its purpose. Racing yachts carry lighter rigging than ocean cruisers to reduce wind resistance and drag, and their masts are of different construction and set up in different ways.

The helm (rudder angle) is tuned while the boat is under way, with the skipper adjusting the sails to reduce factors such as weather and lee helm, so there is minimum use of the rudder and thus minimal drag through the water. More details on tuning for racing are given on p156.

While fine-tuning applies mostly to larger yachts, especially racing yachts, centreboard dinghies also need to be tuned for racing, since the whole purpose behind tuning any type of sailboat is to get the best possible balance between the Centre of Effort and the Centre of Lateral Resistance and thus the best overall performance.

A well-tuned boat is able to maximize the combination of wind in the sails, resistance through the water, and ballast or crew weight, bringing everything into balance and resulting in smooth, fast, forward motion – the key to successful racing.

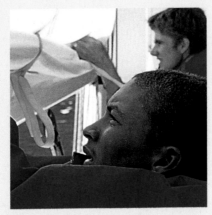

GETTING TO KNOW YOUR BOAT

For most people, buying a boat is a fairly major event which, like buying a house or car, requires careful consideration if problems are to be avoided at the time of purchase or later. There are many factors to consider if you want to ensure that the boat you buy will meet your needs: second-hand versus new, monohull or multihull, racing or cruising design, fibreglass, timber or metal construction and so on. As with any major purchase, advice from experts is important, but much preliminary work can be done by getting to know the various features of each boat. There are many different types of sailboat on the market, and you will have to do your homework before making a choice. The coverage given here will provide an initial guide as to what might be the most suitable sailboat for the purpose you have in mind.

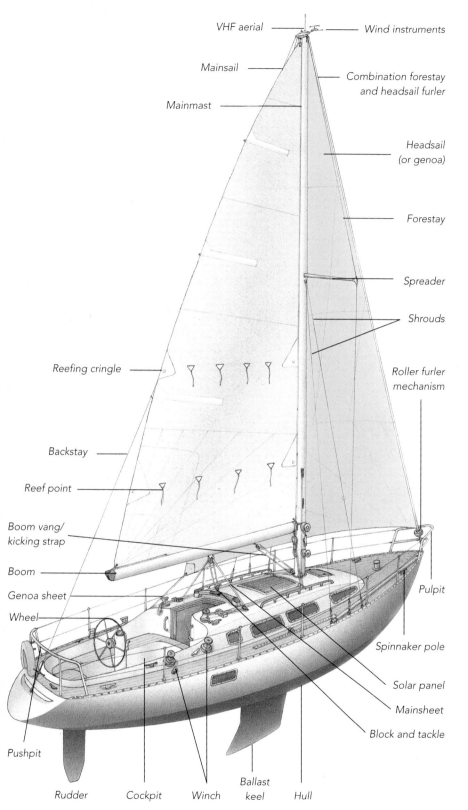

VHF aerial

Wind instruments

Mainsail

Combination forestay
and headsail furler

Mainmast

Headsail
(or genoa)

Forestay

Spreader

Shrouds

Roller furler
mechanism

Reefing cringle

Backstay

Reef point

Boom vang/
kicking strap

Boom

Pulpit

Genoa sheet

Wheel

Spinnaker pole

Solar panel

Mainsheet

Block and tackle

Pushpit

Rudder　　Cockpit　　Winch　　Ballast
keel　　Hull

Ballast keel yachts

A well-built keel yacht is probably the safest type of sailboat afloat. It is virtually impossible to capsize because, the further it is heeled over by the wind, the greater the righting moment of the ballast keel. This, plus the reduced wind pressure in the sails, prevents keel yachts from capsizing in even the strongest winds. Other advantages are seaworthiness (meaning they can be sailed in most sea conditions), and an auxiliary motor, which is essential when the wind dies and you want to get home!

From a cruising perspective, the main advantage is the accommodation. A well-equipped keel boat of moderate size has all the amenities of a holiday house, albeit on a slightly smaller scale, with the added dimension that it can be moved around and anchored in different bays or harbours. This makes it ideal for families; indeed, there is no finer family holiday than a comfortably appointed yacht moored in pleasant surroundings.

However, a deep keel has some disadvantages, notably that the yacht must be moored on a buoy or alongside a jetty or dock. Apart from the ongoing cost, this creates a maintenance problem because the hull, being permanently in the water, is subject to marine growth. This requires the boat to be lifted from the water at least once a year to be cleaned and repainted with special anti-fouling composition.

Small keel yachts that can be transported on a trailer offer a flexible option for weekend sailors with access to different waters.

Above and top: Trailers are used to launch centreboard dinghies from slipways.

Trailer-sailers

Found all over the world, this hybrid design is a compromise between a keel yacht and a centreboard dinghy. Smaller than most keel yachts but larger than an average dinghy, trailer-sailers usually provide limited accommodation in a compact cabin. Since they have retractable centreboard keels they can be run up onto a beach or taken home on a trailer.

In theory, they are the ideal family boat and, in recent years, have enjoyed growing popularity. Being smaller and lighter than a keel boat they are less expensive, and keeping them out of the water on a trailer avoids the problems of mooring and marine growth that plague the owners of larger craft kept permanently in the water.

A factor to keep in mind when considering buying a trailer-sailer is that some models do not have a ballast keel, with the safety and stability this provides. Although those trailer-sailer owners will dismiss this as being irrelevant, claiming that the boat's wide beam, plus correct handling, eliminate the need for ballast, the fact is that, under certain conditions, no matter how well handled, the lack of a ballast keel can make a boat vulnerable to capsize or swamping.

Since trailer-sailers are essentially family boats, the choice of whether or not to have a ballast keel must play a part in any decision-making when comparing this type of boat with others on offer.

Multihulls

Most multihulls are catamarans (two hulls), although there are a few trimarans around. There is a wide variety of twin-hulled craft, ranging from nifty 4–6m (13–20ft) playthings to giant luxury vessels.

Small 'cats' are mostly for fun sailing in calmer waters and they provide great thrills and spills as they hike along at high speed with one float in the air. Like all small craft they are liable to capsize, but for young sailors who enjoy the exhilaration of multihull sailing, that is often half the fun.

Larger cruising catamarans are ideal for tropical and sub-tropical climates in areas where there are lots of islands or reefs, as they can operate in relatively shallow water, have plenty of deck space for sun-worshippers, and can carry extra equipment, such as diving gear. They are popular as charter vessels in places like Australia's Great Barrier Reef or off the cays and islands of the Caribbean, where underwater reefs can restrict the activities of deep keel yachts.

Sleek racing versions of the big multihulls are often entered in lengthy offshore races, particularly in round-the-world races.

Centreboard dinghies

These smallish boats are popular with youngsters as well as the young-at-heart because they provide exciting, exhilarating sailing.

Usually around 2–6m (6ft–18ft) long, they have retractable centreboards instead of ballast keels and are mostly 'class' boats built to a standard design, based on either 'sit in' or 'sit on' models.

Sit-on boats have sealed hulls with an indentation or depression in the deck for the crew. They can be capsized or swamped with no major dramas as they remain watertight and can be easily righted and sailed off again after a capsize.

Sit-in boats are usually open, traditional dinghy designs with thwarts (bench seats) for the crew. Although most carry some form of buoyancy so that they will not sink, once capsized or swamped, they must be righted and bailed out before they can start sailing again.

There is a big following of this type of boat for racing at club and international level, with some dinghy classes represented at the Olympics (see p153).

Single-handed catamarans are great fun for energetic sailors, offering exhilarating sailing when the conditions are right.

Dinghies are an excellent way to acquire basic sailing techniques. Many top racing sailors first learnt to sail in a dinghy.

Sailboat rigs

The rig of a sailboat is designed to suit the purpose for which the boat is used. The fore and aft rig which, as its name suggests, carries the sails in a roughly fore and aft line, is the most widely used rig today

Large, high-performance racing yachts are mostly sloop-rigged, with a jib, and large mainsail set on a single, very tall mast. Handling big sails is no problem for racing yachts with their extensive crews, but cruising yachts are more likely to have limited crews – often just family members – who are not able to handle sails of that size.

For this reason, most family cruising boats have split rigs, comprising a number of smaller sails which, while they may not perform as well as the big, fast rigs, are much easier to handle.

As a general rule, a boat is said to be square rigged if the sails are square shaped and set mainly across the centre line of the boat (the type of rig usually carried by the windjammers of old).

The principal sailboat rigs are depicted below and described opposite:

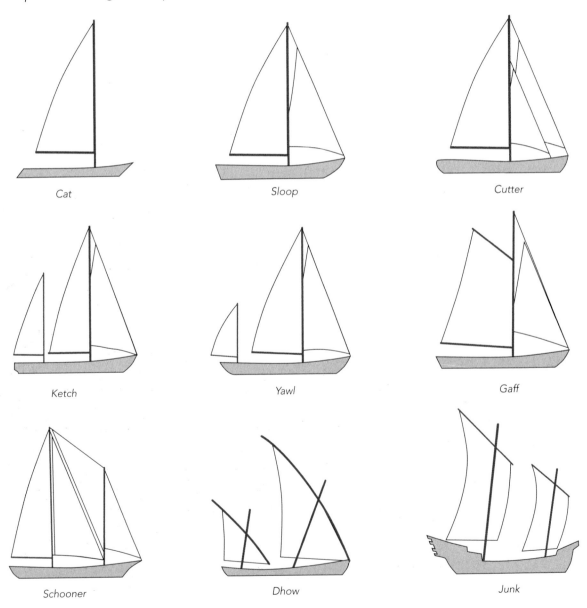

Cat

Sloop

Cutter

Ketch

Yawl

Gaff

Schooner

Dhow

Junk

Cat rig This is the most basic rig, comprising one sail set on the after end of the mast. It is so named because it is a popular rig for catamarans, although many other small craft and centreboard dinghies also use it.

Sloop rig The classic rig for most yachts, consisting of two sails; a mainsail set on the mast and a headsail, or jib, set on the forestay. Different sizes and shapes of jib may have different names; a large overlapping jib is known as a Genoa jib, for example. If both sails run to the top of the mast, the rig is termed a masthead rig, if the jib does not reach to the top of the mast, it is known as a fractional or three-quarter sloop rig.

Cutter rig Much the same as the sloop rig but with two headsails instead of one. A split rig makes sail-handling easy for small crews, making it popular with ocean-going yachts cruising in the trade wind belt, where the winds blow consistently for days on end. When running before the trades, the main is dropped and the headsails are poled out on either side of the boat to create a balanced rig for running downwind with minimum fuss. The inner of the two jibs is called a staysail.

Ketch rig Popular with cruising boats because of its split rig, the ketch rig comprises two masts and three sails. The main mast carries a mainsail and jib in a similar arrangement to a sloop, while the after mast has a smaller sail known as a mizzen. A ketch may also be cutter rigged on the foremast, with the resulting four sails breaking up the rig for even greater ease of handling. The steering position is usually behind the mizzen mast.

Yawl Similar to a ketch in all ways but one; a yawl has its steering position in front of the mizzen mast. As a result, the mizzen is often quite small and used mostly as a steering sail. Yawls can be sloop or cutter rigged.

Gaff rig Still used on some older boats, the gaff rig, once the most popular of all fore and aft rigs for yachts, has been superseded by the sloop rig because the gaff (a boom on the upper edge of the four-cornered sail) was cumbersome and added weight high up on the mast. Gaff sails may be carried with any other rig, so a gaff-rigged cutter or gaff schooner is not uncommon.

Schooner Perhaps the most picturesque of all rigs, the schooner can be rigged in different ways, but is always identified by the foremast being the shorter of its two (or more) masts. The most popular schooner rig is the staysail rig, in which the mainmast is rigged with the standard sloop arrangement and the foremast carries a jib. Between the two masts an inverted triangular sail, known as a fisherman staysail, gives the rig its distinctive appearance. Some schooner rigs have normal fore and aft sails on each mast but, whatever the arrangement, the shorter mast is always in front.

Dhow or lateen rig One of the earliest fore and aft rigs, the dhow or lateen mostly has one sail, although larger vessels may carry two. It consists of a main sail set on a type of gaff or curved boom, which runs from the bow to the top of the mast and often far beyond it. This rig is widely used in the Middle East, particularly in the Arabian Sea and around the Indian Ocean islands.

Junk rig Confined mostly to trading vessels in the Far East, particularly Chinese junks, from whence the name comes. The sails are four-cornered with a gaff and a boom with the leading edge free-flying and not attached to the mast, as are most western rigs. This is not particularly popular as a yacht or pleasure boat rig.

Hull construction

When buying a boat, it is important to know a little about the materials and construction methods used. There are three main boat building materials: GRP (glass reinforced plastic, or fibreglass, a synthetic resin reinforced with fibres or strands of glass), timber (the traditional boat building material), and metal (steel or aluminium). Each has its pros and cons, although GRP is by far the most popular for sailboats of all sizes.

GRP, or fibreglass, is the most popular construction material used in factory-built boats.

GRP (Fibreglass)

Boats constructed of GRP (fibreglass) are usually built in a mould, using layers of polyester resin in which glass fibres are embedded, to create a structure basically similar to reinforced concrete.

Using special spray equipment, the chopped glass strands are sprayed into the mould together with the resin. The laminate is laid up under carefully controlled temperature and humidity conditions and, when cured, the resulting hull is extremely strong.

Smaller craft may be laid up by hand using a fibreglass mat, resembling coarsely woven linen, that is soaked in the polyester resin and pressed into place in the mould.

Different types of resins may be used for different parts of the hull, depending on the finish required. The highly polished finish that makes a boat look so attractive is created by a layer of gel coat resin

that is laid onto the mould before the main laminating resin and glass fibres are added.

The deck and cabin structures are usually laid up in a separate mould, using the same techniques and materials. When the interior of the hull has been fitted out with furniture and fittings, the deck and cabin moulding is lowered into place on the hull and the two are bonded together. The boat is then ready to receive the mast, rigging and other outside fittings.

Timber

Despite having lost some of its appeal, this traditional boat building material is still widely used, especially for small boats. Timber requires a lot of maintenance, however, and boat owners generally prefer to sail rather than carry out chores. A GRP boat only needs to be hauled out of the water once a year for underwater cleaning, but

Timber hulls require a great deal of ongoing maintenance.

timber boats require constant attention to the hull and deck, as the sun and weather take their toll of paint and varnish.

Despite this, many sailors favour timber for its appearance. GRP may be practical but it can look clinical (fibreglass boats are often disparagingly referred to by the timber school as 'plastic bathtubs'). The appealing warm glow of varnished timber on a well-kept vessel is the reason why timber is still widely used, particularly for fitting out cabins and living areas, even on GRP boats.

A timber hull, especially if it is old, means lots of maintenance work. Painted or varnished timber needs fairly constant attention. Even with modern synthetic paints, the sun can play havoc with the appearance of a boat in a very short time, especially in hot climates. It is hard to keep varnish in a pristine condition, so whatever the finish of the timber, its exterior is going to need a considerable amount of work to keep it in top condition.

Timber hulls are subject to the prospect of attack by marine borers (a type of worm). These pests cannot attack fibreglass, but will chew their way into the wetted surface of almost any type of timber boat which is kept in the water. Keeping the anti-fouling composition up to date with fresh coats deters them, but it takes only the smallest area where the composition has been chipped off or missed and toredo worm or some other marine borer will get into the timber and be very difficult to get out. They are often buried deep in the planks and not visible to the naked eye until they have eaten away the timber to the point where the very structure of the boat can be endangered.

Plywood, the traditional material for small boats for many decades, remains popular with amateur boat

Many traditionalists continue to opt for timber-hulled boats, such as this elegant yawl.

builders, especially for sit-in centreboard dinghies and other small yachts. Marine grade plywood is easy to use and relatively inexpensive, making it well-suited to home boat builders, schools and clubs. (Building plans can be obtained from the dinghy class associations.)

These days, most modern racing dinghies are moulded in fibreglass, but there are still many wooden-hulled boats on the water that have stood the test of time.

Metal

Steel appeals to DIY boat-builders with welding skills. Most steel yachts are put together by those looking for a sizeable boat for open water cruising, where the benefits of steel are most advantageous, as sailing among tropical reefs or islands, particularly in the less-charted areas of the Pacific or Indian oceans, can be hazardous, with the ever-present risk of grounding on a coral reef.

Timber or fibreglass boats are easily damaged, whereas a steel hull will bounce off the coral or, at worst, strand on the reef until it can be refloated, often with little damage other than a few dents.

The ability to withstand tough wear and tear is really the only major factor in favour of metal, as it lacks aesthetic appeal and requires considerable maintenance, being very subject to corrosion (and rust streaks down the side of a yacht's hull look very unsightly). Metal is also rather noisy, with the slap of every wave reverberating throughout the hull, as well as the clang of footsteps on deck.

ALUMINIUM

Despite being more resistant than steel to corrosion, aluminium is still aesthetically rather cold and noisy and has never really taken off for yacht construction.

Building with aluminium requires more technical skills than steel, which makes it less popular for home-built boats. However, aluminium is stronger and lighter than steel, and requires relatively little maintenance, provided the correct marine-grade aluminium is used and all the fittings are made from compatible materials. It is widely used for power craft, especially small fishing boats and, when painted, can be as attractive as any other material.

FERRO-CEMENT

Concrete boats (often disparagingly called 'floating pavements'), were popular in the '80s and '90s mainly because of their relatively low cost and ease of construction. Of all the materials suited to home building, reinforced concrete plaster is the easiest for amateur boat builders to use. As a result, hundreds of backyards were turned into boatyards and ferro-cement boats appeared on many of the world's waterways.

Ferro-cement is a form of the reinforced concrete used for building homes and offices, but instead of the heavy steel mesh used in concrete building construction, a light steel mesh, usually chicken wire, provides the reinforcing, as it is easier to shape and form over the steel rods used for the structural makeup of the yacht. A mould is not used; instead, the entire boat is first constructed using the steel rods and chicken wire, and the resulting structure is then plastered over by hand with a special cement mix. In order to get a good finish, a professional plasterer should be called in for the final trowelling.

The deck and cabin are usually built as part of the hull, so the boat is constructed as an integrated structure. The cement surface is then sealed and painted.

An aluminium hull is left unpainted so that any corrosion is soon noticed.

The box structure

The hull of a boat is effectively a box. Although it is sharp at one end and blunt at the other it is still structurally a box. When a box is used for sending something through the mail, it must be strong enough to withstand the stresses and strains of handling. So, while a thin cardboard box is fine for packaging lightweight goodies, it is no good for sending heavy tools through the mail. For this you need a strong, reinforced box.

The same applies to a boat. If it is to be used in quiet water where there will be no great stresses, as is the case with most dinghies, it can be built as a light shell. But if it is to be used in the open seas, where it will encounter big waves and strong winds, it needs to be much stronger and reinforced to withstand the stress it will experience in a seaway.

The structure of every yacht is designed to counter the stresses and strains which are mostly caused by four situations: wracking, hogging, sagging and pounding.

WRACKING

This occurs when the boat goes over a wave at an angle. It also occurs when the boat is running before a sea and the following waves cause it to 'corkscrew' or yaw. Both actions set up a twisting, or wracking, action throughout the hull, creating stresses that can cause severe distortion or damage

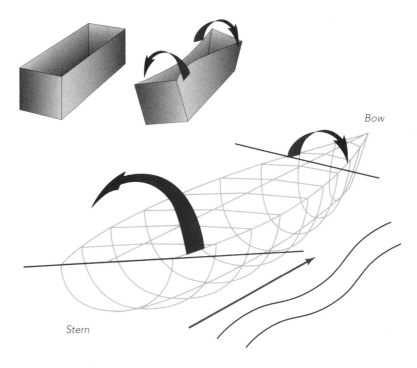

Bow

Stern

The corkscrewing effect of running before a big sea creates the greatest wracking stresses. As a wave lifts under the stern the hull twists one way while the bow, driving into the trough, is forced hard in the other direction.

to the hull. Imagine the cardboard box, mentioned earlier, with each end twisted in opposite directions; that is the sort of action induced by wracking in a seaway.

The reinforcing required to counter wracking stresses is made up of a number of structural members. Deck beams run across the boat from side to side beneath the deck, while bulkheads (which divide the boat into compartments), are located strategically throughout the interior of the hull.

Structural reinforcing in the hull skin ('ribs' in a timber boat), and transverse floors in the bottom of the boat provide added strength to

counter the wracking stresses. A small, but vitally important part of the reinforcing is formed by the join between deck and hull. In timber and metal boats, this reinforcing can be seen as small triangular pieces secured between the underside of the deck and the hull to prevent the sideways movements that occur during wracking. In fibreglass boats, the reinforcing may not be so obvious, but it forms part of the structural makeup of the deck, bulkheads and hull skin.

Whatever the construction, reinforcing is designed to absorb any stresses which might break the bond between deck and hull.

Sagging   Hogging   Pounding

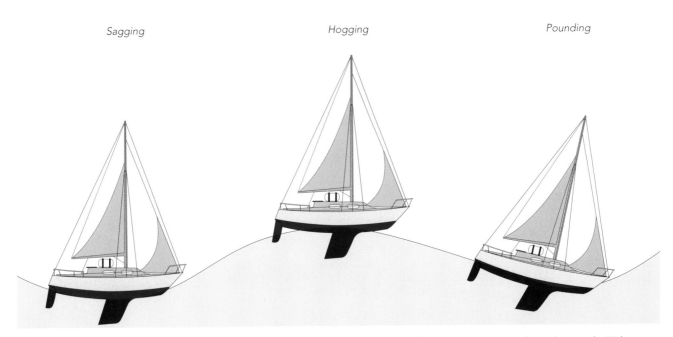

When a boat sags (left), the ends of the hull are supported by two waves, and the midships 'sags' unsupported into the trough. With hogging (centre), as the boat rides over a wave, there is a moment when it is poised on the crest with both bow and stern hanging over the troughs. Pounding (right) is when the underside of the bow takes most of the impact when crashing through a wave into the trough.

Hogging

When a boat rides over the crest of a wave it reaches a point where its centre is supported by the wave while the bow and stern hang in space at each end. Called hogging, this places huge stresses on the boat's structure, with the centre pushed upwards by the wave crest while the ends sag downward, effectively bending the boat over the back of the wave.

If the stresses are not countered, the boat could break in two. While it is unlikely to do this, the enormous stresses induced by hogging can distort and damage the hull structure. To withstand the stress, structural reinforcing, known as stringers, running the length of the boat from bow to stern, provide longitudinal strength. One of the main stringers, known as the keelson, is at the bottom of the hull just above the keel. The deck stringer, or beam shelf, runs along the top of the hull beneath the deck on either side. Further stringers are located between these two to create a strong fore and aft structure which will resist hogging stresses.

Sagging

This is the reverse of hogging. As its name indicates, it occurs when the boat lies between two wave crests and is supported at the bow and stern while the middle sags heavily into the trough. This creates similar longitudinal stresses, which are countered by the same stringers that are used to cope with hogging.

Pounding

When a boat rides over a steep wave it often momentarily poises with the bow in the air before crashing down into the trough. This spine-jarring action, known as pounding, can place enormous strains on much of the boat's structure, particularly the bow.

To counter pounding, the bow is reinforced with strong structural members as well as a solid bulkhead in the eye (peak) of the bow. In most boats, this 'collision' bulkhead separates the bow section of the hull from the main accommodation areas, and creates a small locker which can be accessed from the deck and is often used to store the anchor gear.

Masts, spars and rigging

Sails derive their power from the wind, and the mast, spars and rigging transmit that power to the hull to drive it through the water. While it is obviously important that the mast and rigging are strong enough to withstand the enormous stresses they will encounter, it is also important that they are as light as possible.

This is especially the case with racing boats, where wind drag or excessive weight aloft can noticeably affect a yacht's performance. It is not so critical with cruising yachts, where safety rather than speed is the issue, although excess weight aloft has a detrimental effect on any yacht's stability.

Masts

For most yachts and centreboard dinghies, masts made of extruded aluminium tubing offer the best and cheapest medium on which to mount the sails. They are hollow, with an aerofoil section to reduce wind drag, and the mast wall is as thin as practical to reduce weight. Spars (the boom and spreaders), are usually also made from aluminium. Timber masts are found in older boats, while carbon fibre and similar hi tech materials are used mainly on racing yachts.

The mast may be stepped on deck, or pass through the deck to be stepped on the keel. Nowadays the masts of large craft are mostly stepped on deck, on a reinforced

The mast, spars and rigging, which hold the sails aloft and enable them to be adjusted to suit the wind, are an integral part of the forces that combine to move a yacht.

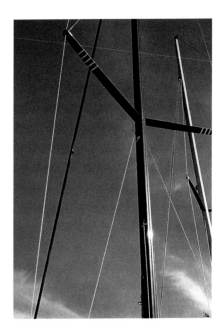

Neatly coiled ropes hanging from a deck-stepped mast.

Aluminium is lightweight and relatively corrosion resistant.

Carbon fibre masts are used mainly on high performance racing yachts.

section of the cabin roof known as the tabernacle. There are two advantages to stepping the mast on deck; firstly it leaves the cabin space below-deck clear and uncluttered (a mast protruding through the middle of the cabin is inconvenient and cumbersome). Secondly, in the unhappy event of losing the mast, a deck-stepped mast falls cleanly over the side and is less likely to tear open the cabin roof as it goes. Stepping the mast on deck also makes maintenance easier for, if the mast has to be dropped, it can be lowered by releasing the rigging, whereas if it is stepped on the keel, a crane will be required to lift it out of the hull.

Mast height is determined by the type of sailing intended. A racing yacht will always have a taller mast than a cruising yacht so it can carry a greater sail area aloft and thus improve performance.

Along the length of the mast are attachment points, or tangs, for the rigging. On the very top, a mast cap secures a number of fittings, from tangs to antennae for sailing and navigation instruments.

Spars

Unlike the old square-rigged ships which had dozens of spars on which their square sails were set, modern fore and aft rigs have very few spars – the boom is usually the only spar of any consequence, its purpose being to provide a solid foot for the mainsail. The boom is connected to the mast by a goose-neck, which allows it to swivel freely, and to the boat by the main sheet, usually close to the after end of the boom.

All racing boats carry at least one spinnaker pole, although this is not a permanent spar, being kept on deck until the spinnaker is used, at which point it is secured to the front of the mast.

The spreaders (also known as crosstrees), might be considered spars, but they are mostly small and attached to the mast at a point or points above the deck. Spreaders are located on either side of the mast and their purpose is to provide a broader angle, and thus better support, between the shrouds (*see standing rigging, opposite*) and the tangs. Cruising yachts normally only carry one set of spreaders, but high performance racing yachts may carry a number because the height and smaller cross section of their masts requires more support.

Rigging

Rigging comes in two forms: standing rigging, the rigid, permanently secured wires that hold the mast in place; and running rigging, usually made of flexible wire or synthetic rope, which is used to hoist and control the sails.

Standing rigging is made from a stiff form of stainless steel wire rope in which a number of strands are twisted together. Flexible wire rope may be of similar construction, but consists of far more strands, allowing it to bend without risk of metal fatigue when used in blocks or tackles.

Except in large yachts, most running rigging uses synthetic rope.

STANDING RIGGING

The mast is held in place by shrouds which run from the side decking to points on either side of the mast, usually beneath the spreaders and at the mast cap. The shrouds are anchored into the hull by chain plates and provide sideways support for the mast. Fore and aft support is by stays; rigid wires that run from the bow and stern to the top of the mast, sometimes to points lower down.

This basic setup allows the mast to be adjusted into the most suitable position, and also permits any tuning that skippers require, such as bending the mast to improve the performance of the sail.

RUNNING RIGGING

The main components of the running rigging are the halyards, which hoist and lower the sails, and the sheets, which control the sails when they are in position. (The term 'sheets' refers to the ropes controlling the sails, and not to the sails themselves.)

Halyards may be of flexible wire rope, but most medium and small yachts prefer synthetic rope, of which there are many types (see p65 for details and uses).

Halyards are mostly run up the inside of the mast from an exit point near the deck and over a sheave or pulley at the masthead. A winch mounted on the mast or cabin top enables tension to be applied to the halyard when the sail is hoisted, for one of the secrets of setting a sail correctly is to ensure it is tensioned correctly. Any slackness in the halyard can affect the performance of the sail.

The sheets are attached to the clew (see p188) of the headsail or spinnaker, and to the underside of the boom for the mainsail. Headsail and spinnaker sheets consist of a rope running from the corner of the sail down either side of the boat through an adjustable sheeting block on the deck and to a winch in the cockpit. The mainsheet controls the boom via a block and tackle secured in or near the cockpit. As a general rule, the skipper handles the rudder and delegates the sheets to his crew.

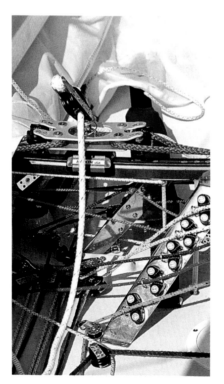

A bosun's chair makes light work of adjusting the standing rigging.

The running rigging, cleats and boom traveller on a racing dinghy.

The sails

Sails are the power unit that drives the boat. To the uninitiated, they may appear to be just sheets of cloth hung from the mast, but a great deal of careful design goes into their cutting and shaping. When wind fills a yacht's sails, they adopt a very hi tech aerofoil shape which converts the power of the wind into forward drive.

Most sails are made from special synthetic materials. Nylon, the first of the synthetics, was initially very popular, but it was inclined to stretch too much, so more suitable synthetic materials, based on polyester, were developed. Terylene and Dacron are two well-known brands, but there are many others, including some specially designed for extreme racing conditions.

Apart from superior performance in use, one of the advantages of synthetic materials is that they are resistant to rot, so sails can be stowed away wet, unlike those made of cotton in days gone by, which had to be dried thoroughly before being stowed away.

Sails are made from different weights of cloth, depending on their intended use. Lightweight cloth is used for light weather sails, particularly for smaller dinghies and sailboards; stronger, coarser material is selected for storm sails, while in between there is a wide range of weights and materials to suit almost every type of sailboat and sailing condition.

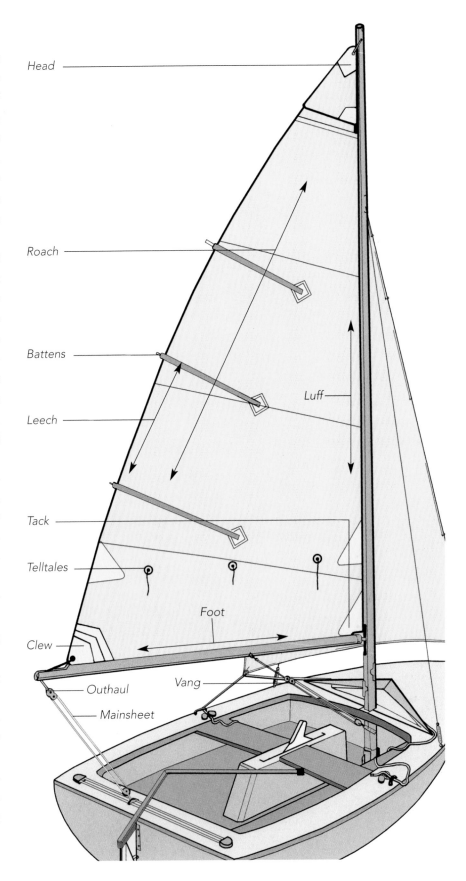

PARTS OF A SAIL

Sails are triangular in shape. The top corner, called the head or peak, is hoisted up the mast by the halyard. The front corner, or tack, is secured to the boom (in the case of the main sail) or the bow (for the jib). The back, or after corner, is the clew. It is to this corner that the controlling sheets are attached, either directly or via the boom.

The leading edge of the sail is the luff, the rear or trailing edge the leech, and the bottom edge the foot, which, in the case of the main, is slotted into a groove on the boom. Both the jib and the mainsail are secured along the luff; the main slotting into the after end of the mast and the jib running up a sleeve on the forestay or clipped onto the forestay at regular intervals along its length with hanks.

A sail plan for an average family sloop is illustrated on the right.

SAIL WARDROBE

The many different types of sails carried aboard a keel yacht are collectively known as the wardrobe.

Centreboarders and day-sailers may carry only the basic jib and mainsail, but ocean-going yachts, in particular high-powered racing yachts, may have 15 or 20 different sails aboard. These would include light weather 'drifters' (big sails made from very lightweight cloth), light weather racing sails, a choice of sails for medium to moderately heavy weather, and heavy-duty

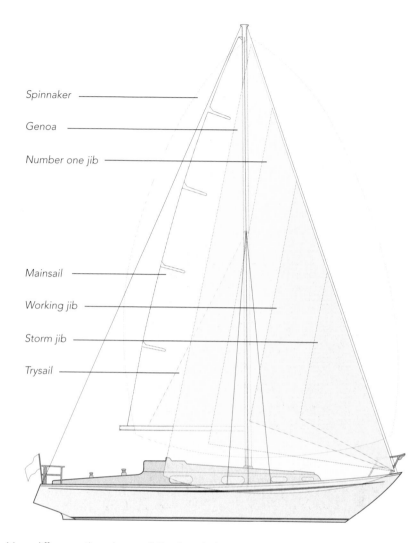

Spinnaker

Genoa

Number one jib

Mainsail

Working jib

Storm jib

Trysail

Many different sails make up a full sail wardrobe; most yacht owners select sails that are the most suitable for the type of boat and the prevailing local weather conditions.

storm sails for use in a blow. Plus, of course, a range of spinnakers to cover all weather conditions.

SETTING THE SAILS

'Bending on' is the term used for attaching the sails to the halyards and sheets in preparation for hoisting. All sails are hoisted with the sheets free and the boat heading into the wind so the sails can flap, otherwise they fill with wind

Repairing a damaged sail.

Crew members drop the jib and raise the spinnaker on a typical round-the-buoys race. The ability to make rapid sail changes really counts in closely fought races.

when halfway up and could jam, or start the boat moving before everything is ready.

Once hoisted, tensioned and secured in place, it is possible to induce different shapes into sails in order to get the best performance in the prevailing wind conditions.

As a general rule, sails are flattened in strong weather by putting maximum tension on the halyard and the outhaul (mainsail), while in light weather they are allowed to 'belly' by easing the tension on both the halyard and the outhaul, which enables them to gather up more wind.

Good sail setting aims to keep the aerofoil shape in the sail as much as possible through all varying wind pressures. When the sail loses this shape, the airflow over the surface is disturbed and the sail will not perform properly. Just as an aircraft will stall if the airflow over its wings is disturbed, a sail will lose its drive the moment it loses a smooth airflow.

To help the skipper determine that the sail is correctly set and the airflow not disturbed, small ribbons, or lengths of wool or cotton, are sewn on either side of the sail to indicate any change in wind

Bending on the mainsail on a dinghy.

flow patterns. When the sail is set correctly and the airflow is smooth, these tufts or 'tell-tales' lie horizontally along the surface of the sail. When the airflow is disturbed they flutter and switch up or down.

An experienced skipper can read how the tufts are moving and know how the sail is performing. He will then adjust the sail's setting, either with the sheets or by turning the boat into or away from the wind, until the tufts are again lying horizontal. Because wind constantly changes direction and strength, such adjustments are made frequently. (See also p43.)

For high-performance racing, various other factors are brought into play to help shape the sails in order to achieve maximum speed advantage under the prevailing wind and sea conditions.

When the tell-tales, or tufts, are horizontal, the boat is pointing at the most efficient angle to the wind. The tell-tales are usually set behind the luff, or leading edge, of the sail.

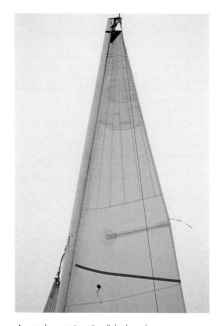

A camber stripe (red) helps the crew to 'read' the sail and trim it effectively.

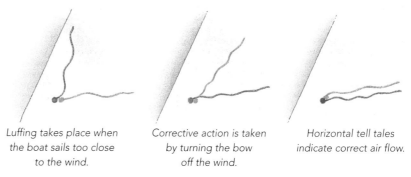

Luffing takes place when the boat sails too close to the wind.

Corrective action is taken by turning the bow off the wind.

Horizontal tell tales indicate correct air flow.

Tell-tales show the airflow over both sides of the sail. By monitoring how they are flying, the helmsman can correct his course to obtain the maximum advantage from the wind conditions. (Here, red depicts windward and green, leeward.)

REEFING

As the wind increases, you might need to reef (shorten or reduce the sail area). In a very heavy blow, smaller storm sails may need to be set. Because changing sails at sea can be taxing on the crew, the first choice is to reduce sail size by reefing. This can be done in a number of ways, all of which have the effect of making the sails smaller without taking them down. Reefing mostly applies to the mainsail, as changing to a smaller headsail (jib) is often easier than trying to reef it.

There are various methods of reefing the mainsail, but slab and roller reefing are the most popular. Slab reefing involves partly lowering the mainsail and tying off the lower section around the boom. A fast method of doing this, termed jiffy reefing, is popular with racing crews as it maintains a fairly good aerofoil shape in the sail.

Roller reefing reduces the sail area by rolling the lower parts of the mainsail around the boom. Although it is simpler than slab reefing, it tends to destroy some of the shape of the sail, so is normally only used when cruising.

When bad weather is on the way, prepare for it by shortening your sails, putting in reefs and checking that everything is secure. It is always better to play safe and reef in good weather. It is better to shake out the reefs later on, than wait until strengthening winds make reefing a dangerous and difficult task. The smaller the crew, the sooner you should reef.

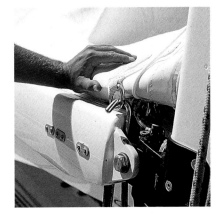

Spinnakers are used when running before the wind in light airs and medium winds. It makes an awesome sight when the whole fleet breaks out their colourful spinnakers, and many top ocean races start with a downwind leg, simply to entertain the spectators.

SPINNAKERS

Sometimes known as 'extras' because they do not set or perform like normal sails, spinnakers are mostly used for racing, partly because they are tricky sails to fly, and partly because they need a large crew to handle them, particularly in fresh winds. They are used when on a broad reach or running before the wind (see p45).

Although some flat-cut spinnakers can be used for reaching; spinnakers can never be used when sailing to windward. They are made of lighter sailcloth than a jib or mainsail and are designed to adopt a full, billowing shape when set, some even appearing like hot-air balloons with their bright colours and patterns.

Deck gear

The deck of a yacht is the main working area and carries a lot of equipment related to the handling of the boat, as well as the safety of the crew. The entire deck area is enclosed with safety rails (guardrails), beginning at the bow with solid stainless steel rails (the pulpit) to which are attached stainless steel wires (often plastic-covered) that run down either side of the boat to a solid rail arrangement at the stern, which is not unlike the pulpit and is called the pushpit. The wires are tensioned with turn-buckles (lashings) or rigging screws to create a ring of steel around the deck, providing good protection for crew moving around or working on deck. On the foredeck, the rails may be interlaced with lifelines made from cord or fine rope, to further protect crew.

The anchor gear, located at the tip of the bow, is important for general purposes and for safety. The anchor warp (rode) is normally stowed in a locker at the bow. The anchor may be similarly stowed, or securely lashed to the deck. (Anchors are described on p71.)

The spinnaker pole is also lashed onto the foredeck so it is close at hand when the spinnaker is used.

A hatch situated somewhere forward of the mast, and leading into the below decks area, provides both light and ventilation. It is also used to facilitate handling the headsails, spinnakers or any other gear that might be needed on the foredeck. Since the sails and much of the equipment is kept below decks, the forward hatch eliminates the need to drag wet sails and other wet or bulky items through the cabin.

Parts of the foredeck

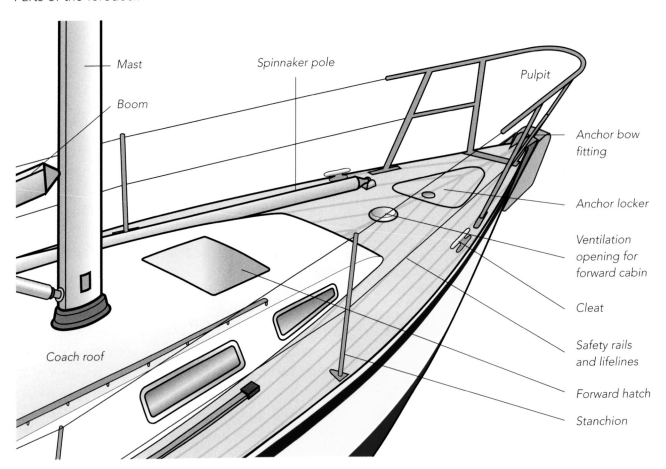

Mast

Boom

Spinnaker pole

Pulpit

Anchor bow fitting

Anchor locker

Ventilation opening for forward cabin

Cleat

Safety rails and lifelines

Forward hatch

Stanchion

Coach roof

Parts of the cabin top (coach roof)

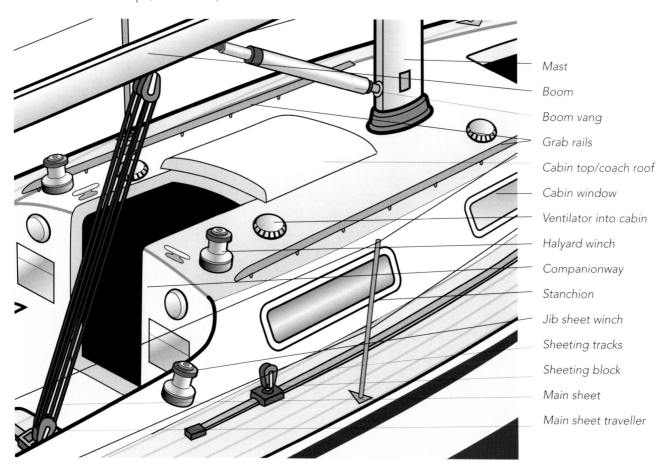

Mast

Boom

Boom vang

Grab rails

Cabin top/coach roof

Cabin window

Ventilator into cabin

Halyard winch

Companionway

Stanchion

Jib sheet winch

Sheeting tracks

Sheeting block

Main sheet

Main sheet traveller

The mast will most probably be stepped on the cabin top (also called the coach roof). At the base of the mast, a number of sheaves and blocks lead the various pieces of running rigging from their exit box at the foot of the mast to the winches in the cockpit and/or on the cabin top.

Usually bolted to the deck on either side of the boat and running aft are the sheeting tracks for the headsail. These enable the sheeting blocks (which lead the sheets from the sails to the cockpit) to be moved in order to maintain the correct angle between the sheets and the sail, an important factor in obtaining good sail shape.

In performance racing-boats, the tracks can be quite long, and sometimes two tracks are carried to enable the sheeting angle to be varied according to the wind conditions and the sails being carried.

On some boats the main sheet is located on the cabin top, although more often it is attached to a track, called a traveller, in the cockpit or immediately behind it. The boom vang (kicking strap) which restricts the boom from riding up when the main sheet is eased, and helps to prevent an accidental gybe (see p49), is located somewhere on the cabin top near the mast, as are the handrails (grab rails) which provide security for crew working on deck when the boat is moving around in a seaway.

The main hatch into the interior of the boat, called the companion way, is situated at the end of the cabin. Ventilators for fresh air are located at different points across the cabin top. If an inflatable life raft is carried, it is usually secured to the cabin top.

Parts of the cockpit

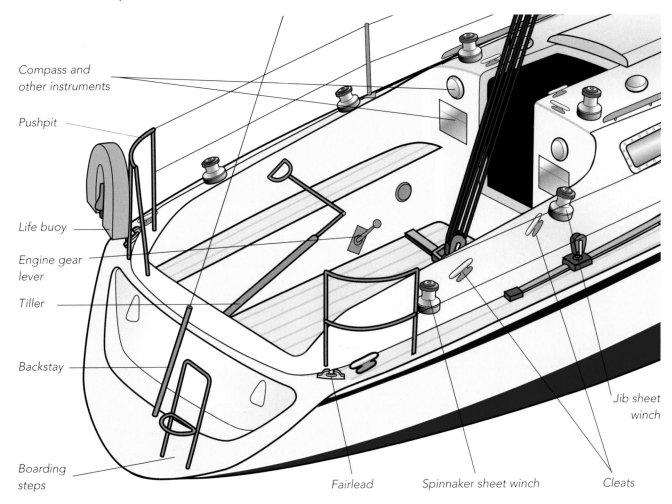

Compass and
other instruments

Pushpit

Life buoy

Engine gear
lever

Tiller

Backstay

Boarding
steps

Jib sheet
winch

Fairlead   Spinnaker sheet winch   Cleats

The cockpit is the boiler room of the yacht, and all the controls are located here. The tiller, or steering wheel, is the dominant feature, together with a fixed compass and a bank of wind and navigation instruments. The instrument panel is located somewhere in front of the helmsman so that he can keep his eye on wind shifts and the speed of the boat.

Big sheet winches are located on either side of the cockpit coaming (the raised frame around the cock-pit edge to keep out the water) so the crew can remain within the cockpit while tending the headsail (jib) and spinnaker sheets.

The cockpits of most yachts are self-draining, allowing any water that gets into the area to quickly drain off. This is particularly important at sea, where a boarding wave could swamp the cockpit, creating a safety hazard if it is not immediately drained away.

There is normally not much deck space behind the cockpit, but what there is may carry instrument antennae, and a variety of items, such as life buoys and dan buoys, which need to be close at hand or cannot be stowed below. A small hatch is usually located near the stern for stowing bailing buckets, ropes, fenders and other items used only occasionally.

(Deck gear varies from boat to boat, according to the designer's brief or the skipper's preference.)

Marine motors

While the sailing purist may scorn motors in a sailboat, the fact is that there are times when a motor is not just a useful asset, but an important safety factor. Many a sailor has thanked his lucky stars for the diesel power that got him back to harbour when the mast and sails had gone over the side, or enabled him to recover a man overboard in a seaway before he was lost among big seas.

Even more sailors have been grateful to just get back to port when the wind had died and they were facing the prospect of an uncomfortable night on the ocean. So, although they perhaps do not fit comfortably into the basic sailing environment, motors are an important part of safety at sea.

Marine motors come in a range of shapes and sizes. Day sailers and small family yachts can get by with an outboard hung on the stern, and centreboard dinghies can be made into fun family fishing boats by fitting a small outboard motor to the transom. But larger boats, especially those that sail offshore, need a solid motor that will punch into a sea if need be, and can run continuously for a long time. This requires an inboard motor – the maritime version of a car engine.

Marine inboard motors need to be specially adapted to cater for the different conditions encountered in a boat, mostly in relation to the cooling system, as salt water

A marine diesel engine is specially manufactured for use in water. If you maintain your engine properly, it should be there for you if you ever need it in an emergency.

causes severe corrosion problems in marine engines.

As with vehicles, marine motors can be fuelled by either diesel or petrol, with diesel being the preferred fuel since it does not require the electrics that are essential for petrol-powered motors. Like the cooling system, the electrical system can soon become corroded in the salt-laden atmosphere that is usually present on a boat.

Since auxiliary motors are often quite small, they are not expensive to run, and using diesel fuel also reduces the fire risk which is always present with petrol.

Installing a boat's motor is a job for a marine engineer as the engine must be correctly aligned

and fitted onto a structural base that can transmit the propeller thrust into the hull structure.

Approved fuel tanks must be equipped with breather pipes which exhaust (vent) to the outside air, and gas detectors (sniffers) installed in the bilges to detect any leak which might create a fire or explosion hazard.

A complete switchboard system caters for the electrical circuits for the lights, motors and auxiliary power requirements, such as CD players or navigation equipment. Most yachts rely on a 12-volt battery system for lighting and power, and carry a double bank of heavy-duty batteries which are regularly charged from the motor.

SAILING TECHNIQUES

In order to get the best performance from a boat, different handling techniques for different types of sailing are necessary. Unlike a car, where you can just get in, start the motor and drive away, a sailboat requires certain sail settings, handling techniques and frequent adjustments to make it sail properly. Because the wind, tide and other factors vary all the time, these handling techniques change as the boat is sailed from place to place. Knowing the idiosyncrasies of your boat and handling it correctly to counter changing conditions is a vital part of good sailing. Although basic sailing techniques are necessary for good sailing at any time, they are particularly important when racing.

Setting the sails

A boat cannot sail directly into the wind as this will result in the airflow down both sides of the sail being equal, which will cause the sail to flap and lose the all-important aerofoil shape which drives the boat forward (see pp 12, 34). If the bow is turned away from the wind, the sails will fill on one side, the aerofoil shape will be restored, and the boat will move forward again.

An average cruising boat can sail up to an angle of about 45 degrees on either side of the wind. Inside that is a non-sailing ('no-sail') zone (see p45). To make progress into the wind, the boat must zigzag with the wind at around 45 degrees first on one side then the other, a procedure known as beating (a term for working the boat, or tacking, upwind. See also p47).

Sailing across the wind or down wind is much simpler; the boat is pointed in the required direction and the sails set accordingly.

LUFFING

The luff, or front edge of the sail, provides the first indication that a sail is not set correctly. If the wind begins to get around the lee side, the luff will start to quiver, a condition known as luffing. Unless this is corrected, the sail will start to collapse and the boat will lose power.

The first corrective action is to tighten the sheets. If the sheets are already hard on and the luffing continues, the boat is sailing too

These boats are sailing on a broad reach, away from the wind (see p45).

close to the wind, within the no-sail, or no-go zone (see p45). A second correction is then applied by turning the bow away from the wind. This latter action is always taken when tacking, because heading a boat into the wind requires the sails to be pulled on as tightly as possible, so luffing can only be corrected by turning the bow off the wind. (See also p35.)

In all other sailing positions, easing the sheets out as far as they can go without luffing achieves maximum drive from the sail.

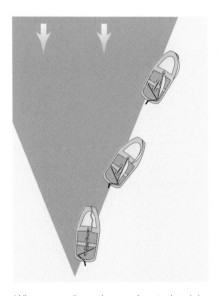

When you sail too close to the wind and the sails start to luff, first pull the sheets on hard, then turn your bow off the wind to regain speed.

A yacht performs at its best when it is sailed on the designed waterline. Sailing is about maximizing a boat's performance in conjunction with the influence of the wind and waves.

TRIMMING THE BOAT

The hull of a yacht is designed to produce maximum performance when it is sailed on the designed waterline. If it is trimmed with the bow or stern up in the air, it will not be on the level waterline and, rather like a car with a flat tyre, will move but will not perform well. Trimming the boat is therefore very important, especially in the fore and aft direction for, although it will naturally heel to one side with the pressure of the wind in the sails, the designer allows for this. Even so, heeling should be kept to a minimum, as performance is always enhanced when the boat is reasonably upright.

Trimming is mostly done with ballast, of which there are three main types: water, weights and human bodies! Crack ocean-racing yachts often use water ballast which can be pumped in and out of tanks to trim the boat according to prevailing conditions, but most cruising yachts use lead or some other heavy weight permanently secured in the keel or bilges.

Centreboard dinghies, having no fixed ballast, use the body weight of their agile crews to swing out on the gunwale or in a trapeze to counter the heel and bring the boat back as much as possible to the upright. Racing yachts also use human ballast; moving their numerous crew members up onto the weather gunwale to achieve the same effect.

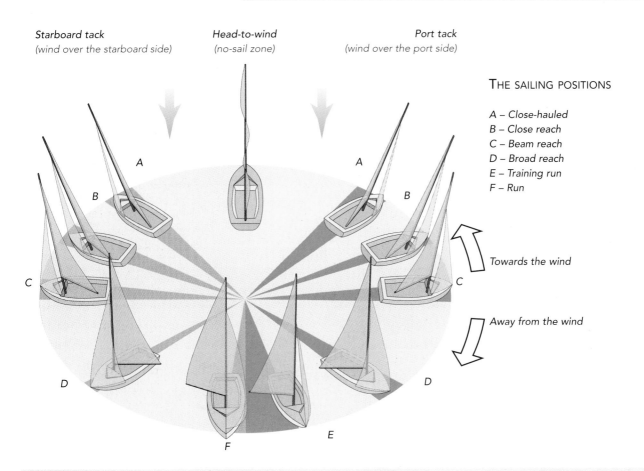

Starboard tack
(wind over the starboard side)

Head-to-wind
(no-sail zone)

Port tack
(wind over the port side)

THE SAILING POSITIONS

A – *Close-hauled*
B – *Close reach*
C – *Beam reach*
D – *Broad reach*
E – *Training run*
F – *Run*

Towards the wind

Away from the wind

The sailing positions (Points of sailing)

Close-hauled (beating) A boat sailing as close to the wind as possible, without luffing, is said to be close-hauled, a term which indicates how the sails should be set – hauled in as close as possible.

Close (shy) reach In this sailing position the boat is not quite close-hauled. The wind is neither ahead, nor on the beam (coming across the side of the boat), so the sails are eased a little from the close-hauled position, as far as they will go without luffing.

Beam reach When sailing at right angles to the wind, a boat is said to be reaching. Since the wind is on the beam (about halfway between ahead and astern), the sails are set approximately halfway out. The exact setting is achieved with the sails eased out as far as possible without luffing.

Broad reach When the wind is abaft (behind) the beam, but not right astern, the boat is said to be broad reaching. The sails are eased out to the point where luffing begins, then taken in enough to kill the luffing. In this position the wind is fairly well astern and it may be possible to hoist a reaching spinnaker.

Run With the wind coming from behind the boat, sail setting is straightforward. The sails are simply spread out as far as they will go to catch as much wind as possible, and the boat runs free before the wind. When the wind is dead astern, the jib may collapse if it becomes blanketed by the main. In this case, it can either be pulled across to the opposite side where it will fill again, or it can be lowered and replaced by a spinnaker. (Full sized parachute spinnakers can only be used when running free.)

In order to beat to windward (sail upwind) the sails must be sheeted in hard to minimize luffing and obtain maximum forward movement. Efficient sail trimming on this, as on all other points of sailing, is the key to optimum sailing performance.

Sail trim

It is the job of the sheet-hands to ensure that the sails are always set for maximum performance. This means keeping a constant eye on the luff of each sail and trimming it accordingly. Each time the boat alters course, the sails need to be reset and trimmed, to keep them performing at full capacity; similarly, they must be adjusted for every change in wind direction. If a sail luffs, the boat loses speed so, particularly in racing, the sheet hands must be ready to adjust the sheets at the first shimmer of the luff.

Adjustments should be made smoothly and in conjunction with any alteration of course. When the boat bears away from the wind, the sails are eased as it turns, so that when it takes up the new course, they can be set as far out as possible without luffing. When the boat closes up on the wind, the sheets are brought on during the turn to prevent even the first signs of any luffing.

In this way the boat is able to manoeuvre at full power the whole time, with both sails drawing to their maximum.

CENTREBOARD ADJUSTMENT

Small sailing dinghies with centre-boards can improve their performance on different points of sailing by adjusting the centreboard.

When sailing into the wind, the maximum lateral resistance is required, so the centreboard must be fully lowered. However, with the wind astern (coming from behind) no lateral resistance is required, so the centreboard can be fully raised. Anywhere between these two situations, the centreboard must be adjusted to match the sailing position.

Tacking

When the wind comes across the port side, a boat is said to be sailing on a port tack; with the wind on the starboard side, it is sailing on a starboard tack. To make progress into the wind, as described on p43, it must zigzag, first on one tack then the other – this is known as tacking, or beating, to windward.

Changing from one tack to the other can be done either by bringing the boat up to and through the wind so that the wind crosses the bow (going about), or by heading the boat away from the wind, so that the wind is brought across the stern (gybing, see p49).

Tacking, or going about, involves taking the boat's bow through the no-sail zone, from close-hauled on one tack to close-hauled on the other. In order to get through the no-sail zone, where the sails will be ineffective and the boat will slow down, it must first be brought up to the close-hauled position to gain enough speed to carry it through the no-sail zone (see p45).

THE PROCEDURE FOR TACKING (GOING ABOUT) IS AS FOLLOWS:

1. *'Sheet on!'* This command is given by the skipper as he brings the boat up to the close-hauled position. Both jib and main sheets are brought on hard. This not only gets the boat into position, ready to change tack, but also increases the speed.

2. *'Ready about!'* A warning to everyone on board that the boat is about to change tack. The jib sheet-hand on the weather side picks up the loose sheet on that side and takes a couple of turns around the winch. The sheet-hand on the lee side prepares to release his jib sheet. The main sheet remains pulled on tight throughout the manoeuvre.

3. When the crew is ready, the skipper shouts *'Lee oh!'* or *'Helm a-lee!'*, then puts the helm down and steers the boat up into and across the wind at maximum speed. The sails will flap violently as the wind comes directly ahead.

4. This means the boat has crossed through the wind, so the previously tight weather-jib sheet is released and the opposite sheet taken on and winched in tight. In this way, as soon as the manoeuvre is completed, the jib will fill with wind and drive the boat forward again before it loses too much speed.

5. Once on the new tack, the helm is straightened and the jib sheet secured in the close-hauled position as the boat sails off on the next leg.

Going about in small centreboard boats follows the same procedure, but without winches and with the centreboard fully down.

Push the tiller away from you in order to push the bow into the eye of the wind.

As the boom comes across the centre line, move to the other side, keeping the tiller over until the tack is complete.

Cross to the windward side, and centre the tiller to begin sailing on the new tack.

In irons

If the boat is too slow in turning and fails to cross the no-sail zone, it will stall with its head (bow) to wind; a position known as 'in irons' or 'in stays'. This is a dangerous situation because the boat is out of control. To get it out of irons and back under control, the jib can be reversed (backed) to push the bow away from the wind so the boat can resume its former sailing position, get up some speed and try again. Catamarans (multihulls) can easily find themselves in irons, so they need to gain a lot of speed before attempting to go about.

This boat has found itself in irons, or facing directly into the wind – the equivalent of a motor car stalling. To get going again, push the tiller away from you and pull the jib to the opposite side (called backing the jib) so that the sail catches the wind on it's 'back' side.

Beating

Since the average cruising boat sails at about 45 degrees to the wind, beating to windward (sailing upwind or close-hauled) means tacking (changing course) through roughly 90 degrees on each leg. In theory, if the boat were to remain on one tack until the windward destination was at right angles to its course, the next tack would take it directly there. In practice it does not work quite that way because other factors come into play, notably leeway (the drift of the boat with the wind), the likelihood of wind shifts, proximity of shorelines, etc. A skipper will soon get to know just how close to the wind his boat will sail, and therefore when to make each tack.

Efficient beating is important in both racing and cruising. In racing it is crucial, since a lot of time, and thus the race, can be lost by slow or incorrect tacking. In cruising it is not so important, but it can still be frustrating when the boat makes a whole series of tacks, yet seems to make little progress into the wind.

Beating requires special skills on the part of the skipper. Running too far on one leg will add extra distance, while tacking too soon will require extra tacks, and thus slow the boat.

There are other factors which can inhibit the boat's progress when beating. The lee of headlands must be avoided, while tidal effects must be assessed and the most beneficial flow utilized. In busy harbours, commercial traffic can also interfere with the planned tacking route.

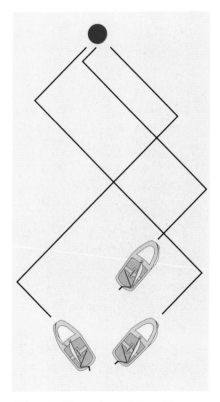

Although different boats follow different tacks (zigzag courses), they end up at the same windward point.

Gybing

This involves changing tack with the wind across the stern. It can be quite a dangerous manoeuvre in strong winds and must be done with care, otherwise the boat can be damaged or crew injured. The danger comes from the mainsail and boom flying from one side of the boat to the other in an uncontrolled gybe. Ideally, the boom must be helped across by pulling it in and then letting it out slowly on the other side in order to reduce the impact.

In small centreboard craft, an accidental or poor gybe will almost certainly result in a capsize.

THE PROCEDURE FOR GYBING IS AS FOLLOWS:

1. *'Ease sheets!'* As he gives this order, the skipper steers the boat away from the wind to a point where it is almost directly astern and the sails are right out. The jib will probably collapse behind the mainsail.

2. *'Ready to gybe!'* This is the warning to all on board that the boat is about to gybe. Those in the cockpit need to keep their heads down! The jib sheet-hand carries out the same procedure as for tacking, but does not pull the jib tight when it changes sides, as the boat will still be running free after the gybe. The boom vang is hauled tight and secured to prevent the boom rising and bringing on an accidental gybe.

3. At this point the main sheet-hand is in control. He has to help the boom across from one side to the other, avoiding the sudden rush and heavy impact that can occur when the wind gets round to the other side of the sail, and which can harm both boat and crew. When all is ready, the helmsman steers the boat away from the wind, putting the stern into and across the wind. The sheet-hand pulls in the main sheet as fast as possible.

4. *'Gybe oh!'* As the wind gets round to the other side, and the boom flies across the boat, he quickly lets the main sheet run out to absorb the impact.

5. When the gybe is over, the helm is centred and the sails reset for the next course.

Centreboard dinghies do not pull in the main sheet and let it run out; they just let the boom flick over from one side to the other, as their gear is lighter and less likely to do any damage. If the boom is not released fast enough, the impact of the gybe will probably capsize the boat in strong weather.

When preparing to gybe, pull the tiller towards you, controlling the main sail with the main sheet as it crosses the boat.

Move across the boat, making sure that you don't sheet the main too hard on the new reach.

Swap your tiller and mainsheet hands, and settle down on your new course.

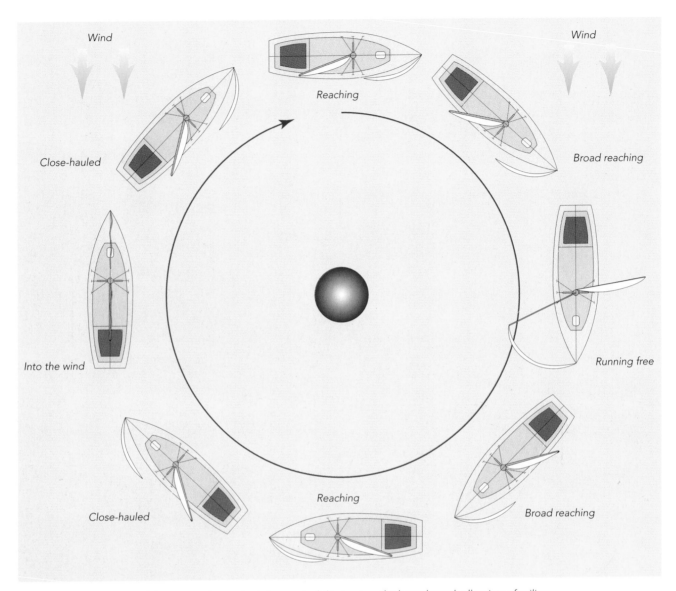

Sailing in a circle, or 'around the compass' tests the helmsman's ability to steer the boat through all points of sailing.

Sailing in a circle

When a boat sails on a straight course, the sails are set for that sailing position (as far out as possible without luffing), and only adjusted if there is a change of wind direction.

Since both racing and cruising involve sailing on many different courses, it is important to learn to combine the various sailing positions in order to take the boat in any direction required.

A good training technique is to take the boat out into clear water and sail it in a circle, which incorporates every point of sailing (see p45) and is the basis on which all sailing manoeuvres are built.

The simple triangular course, around which most short races are run (see p159), is an adaptation of the sailing circle, and is intended to test the participants on all points of sailing in the course of the race.

As a full sailing circle involves the use of all the basic sailing positions, any boat can be sailed in any direction simply by adopting one of these manoeuvres.

The exercise can be repeated in either a clockwise or an anticlockwise direction by using the same actions in a different sequence.

THE PROCEDURE FOR SAILING IN A CIRCLE IS AS FOLLOWS:

1. Set the boat sailing close-hauled on a starboard tack.
2. *'Ready about!'* Helm down.
3. *'Lee oh!'* The boat tacks across the wind.
4. *'Sheets on!'* Straighten the rudder, the boat is now close-hauled on a port tack.
5. Helm up. *'Ease sheets!'* The boat bears away from the wind until it is reaching. Sails are adjusted for the reaching position, roughly half way out.
6. Helm up again. *'Ease sheets!'* The boat bears away more until it is running free on the port tack with the wind astern.
7. *'Ready to gybe!'* Helm up and the boat gybes the stern through the wind.
8. *'Gybe oh!'* The gybing manoeuvre is carried out. The sheets are run right out and the boat is now running free on the starboard tack.
9. Helm down. *'On sheets!'* The boat is brought up towards the wind and sails are adjusted to the reaching position.
10. Helm down. *'On sheets!'* The boat is brought up more into the wind and the sheets are brought hard on until it is close hauled on the starboard tack.

The rear boat is beating to windward. It will soon tack and ease into a reach (the position already reached by the right-hand boat), then ease further into the running position already achieved by the front boat (on the left of the picture).

These boats are rounding the windward mark. As they do so, they will fall away to port and ease out the sheets to go on either a reach or a run.

Manoeuvring around a busy marina can be testing for a novice skipper, but with practice it becomes easier. It is preferable to use a motor under these conditions, but a competent sailor will also be able to manoeuvre under sail if his engine fails.

Basic sailing manoeuvres

Having mastered the basic controls of a car, a learner driver then starts to develop his skills in terms of parking, three-point turns, starting on a hill, and so on. Similarly, when a novice sailor has learned to handle the boat through the basic sailing positions, he can start putting them into practice in more advanced manoeuvres. A dinghy sailor, for example, needs to learn how to sail his boat on and off a beach, while a keelboat skipper may need to learn how to sail his boat onto a mooring.

These mostly commonplace procedures require only the basic boat handling skills described earlier in this chapter but, because of the conditions that can sometimes exist, such as strong winds or shallow water for the centreboarder, or unfavourable, gusty winds around a yacht's moorings, these basic skills should be developed until handling the boat in any situation, under any weather or water conditions, becomes second nature.

SAILING ONTO A MOORING

This is one of the more frequently used sailing manoeuvres. Many, if not most, yachts tie up to a mooring at least occasionally and, while it is prudent in a crowded waterway or in difficult conditions to pick up the mooring under power, sailing up to the mooring can make an impressive spectacle if done right. In any case, it is a useful skill to acquire against the time when the motor does not work.

Done correctly, mooring under sail should not involve any great risk to the boat or other vessels in the anchorage, although it does require a degree of skill, depending on the wind conditions.

The boat must be manoeuvred into a suitable position downwind of the mooring buoy, then rounded up directly into the wind so that it gradually loses speed and drifts up to the buoy.

It is important to know how far the boat carries after being rounded up into the wind, for at this point the sails will be flapping and it will lose power. The skipper must learn to judge his approach accurately because, if the boat overshoots the mooring buoy it will mean getting it under way again and going round for another attempt. If the boat undershoots, it will stall in the midst of a crowded mooring area – not a pleasant situation at any time.

The best approach is to sail across wind on a reach to the rounding-up position downwind of

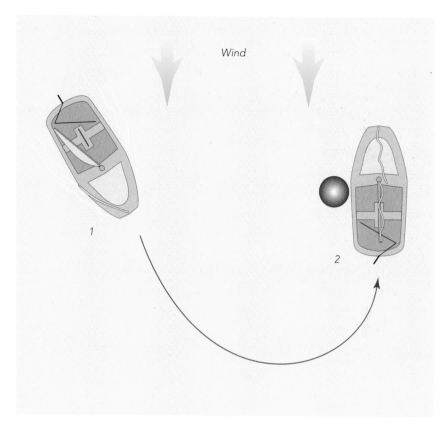

To pick up a mooring under sail, using only a jib, sail on a broad reach to a position downwind of the mooring (1). When you reach the rounding-up position, gently luff up (turn to face the wind) and release the jib in order to drift to a stop alongside the mooring (2).

the mooring buoy. A reach allows for an adjustment of course and speed right up to the last moment, whereas sailing close-hauled or running free does not offer the same latitude. When the rounding-up position is reached, the boat is turned head to wind and the sails released. ('Let fly!' is a term often used for this.)

With the sails flapping, the boat carries its momentum into the wind, gradually slowing as it approaches the mooring until, if the manoeuvre has been carried out successfully, the boat stops alongside the buoy, which is then lifted aboard.

Judging the distance for rounding up is the secret to successful mooring under sail. Since this will vary with the strength of the wind and the way the boat handles, it requires some skill and expertise before it becomes second nature.

The danger with either under- or over-shooting is that the boat will be temporarily out of control and it will take a few minutes to get sailing again. The close proximity of other moored craft can make this a somewhat hazardous situation. This is where the crew may be needed on deck to fend off any possible collisions.

SAILING OFF A MOORING

This is an easier and less hazardous procedure than sailing onto a mooring, because the boat can remain secured to the buoy until it is under full control and starting to sail. It can even be headed off in the required direction in order to avoid other boats moored in close proximity. The sails are hoisted with the sheets free. Since boats generally lie head to wind on a mooring, the sails will flap and the boat will not attempt to move.

The crew are briefed on which tack they will sail off; when everyone is ready, the forward hand crew disconnects the mooring line from the bow cleat and walks it back down the deck on the side the boat is to sail off. As he does so, the bow will swing off the wind in the planned direction, although the boat it will not move, because the sails are still free and flapping.

When the mooring has been brought back to the point where the boat is heading in the required direction – the reaching position is best – the mooring is released, the sheets pulled on, and the boat will move off on the desired tack and under full control.

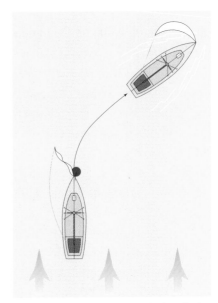

Wind aft of the beam: Hoist the headsail and immediately drop the mooring (or raise the anchor). Sail well clear before hoisting the mainsail.

To sail away close-hauled, the crew releases the mooring near the bow.

To sail away on a close reach, the crew releases the mooring amidships.

To sail away on a reach, the helmsman releases the mooring astern.

The effect of tides on mooring and berthing

The sailing manoeuvres in this chapter have been described without mentioning the effect of tide and tidal streams yet, in some parts of the world, tides can have almost as much effect on the boat as wind (see p103).

It is impossible to describe all the methods available to counteract the tidal movements that may be encountered while mooring, anchoring or berthing, since tides vary not only from waterway to waterway, but even from place to place within a waterway. The best solution is to acquire local knowledge, either from personal experience or by taking advice from helpful locals.

Coastal areas may sometimes be covered by local tidal flow charts but, as a general rule, these cover movements only of the main body of water and, outside the main stream, tidal flow is often unpredictable, with counter-currents and eddies creating big problems for boats that are not familiar with the particular area.

A moored boat will face into the strongest element. If it faces into the wind, it is described as wind-rode (A), but if it is facing into the tide it is tide-rode (C). If the wind and tide are in opposite directions, the boat will lie head to whichever element, either wind or tide, is the strongest (B).

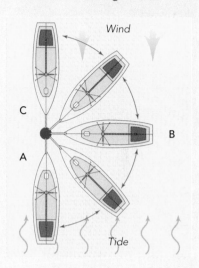

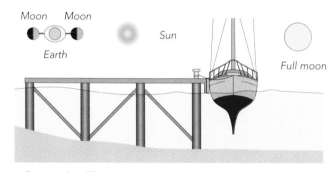
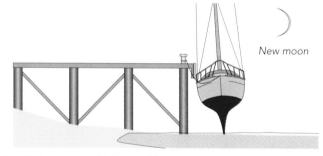

Spring tides: The sun and moon pull together at full or new moon, when high waters are highest and low waters are lowest.

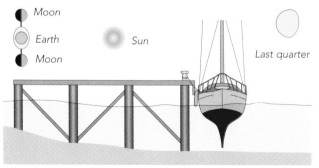
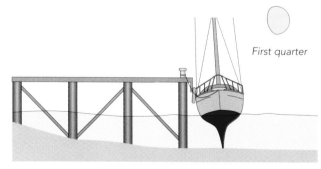

Neap tides: The moon pulls at right angles to the sun when the former is in its first or last quarter. Tides are moderate, with high waters at their lowest level and low waters at their highest level.

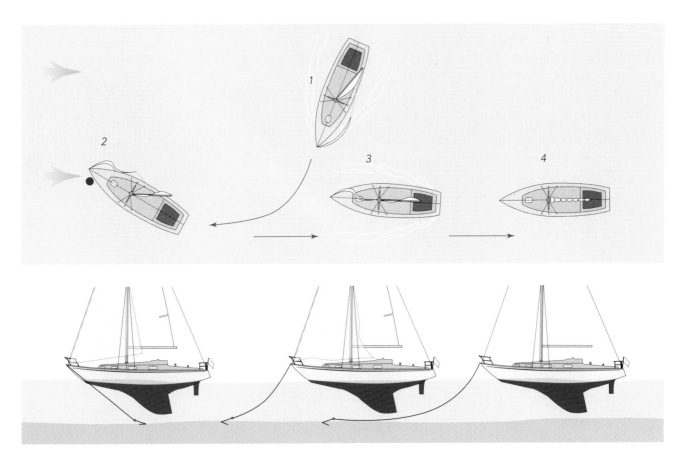

To anchor a yacht under sail, luff up as soon as you reach your anchoring point (1) until the boat stops with the sails free and flapping. As the boat drifts back, drop the anchor (2), leading the warp through the bow fairlead, having first secured the free end. Once you feel the anchor take, lower the mainsail (3). Finally, test the anchor and take a transit bearing (see p74). When you have established your bearings and are satisfied the anchor will hold, the jib can be lowered (4).

ANCHORING UNDER SAIL

This manoeuvre is almost identical to that of sailing onto, or picking up, a mooring under sail (see p53).

First, select a suitable spot for dropping the anchor, bearing in mind the need to have adequate manoeuvring room downwind of it, and the fact that the boat will fall back on the rode or warp once the anchor has been dropped (this is particularly important if there are other vessels in the anchorage).

The anchor is prepared on the bow (see p73) and the boat lined up for a cross-wind (reaching) approach. Since there is no buoy to pick up, judging the distance for rounding up is not so critical, as the anchor can be dropped as soon as the boat loses way and stops.

When the boat is downwind of the chosen position, it is rounded up head to wind with all sails free and flapping, losing way slowly, as when picking up a mooring buoy.

When the boat stops, the anchor is dropped. The boat's head will fall off the wind as it starts to drop back on the anchor rode (see p188), which is paid out until the predetermined anchorage point is reached. The anchor is then snubbed up on the bow cleat and secured. If the anchor takes, the boat will pull up and swing round to lie head to wind on the rode.

It is not advisable to drop all the sails until the boat has been firmly brought up for, if the anchor drags, the boat may have to be sailed off for another attempt. In a crowded anchorage, you may not be able to raise the sails fast enough, which could prove dangerous.

WEIGHING ANCHOR UNDER SAIL

This is a slightly different procedure to that used when sailing off a mooring, because the anchor warp cannot be walked back to the cockpit. The anchor will be well dug-in to the sea bed and the boat must be directly above, or almost above, the anchor before it can be plucked out.

With the sails hoisted and free so they can flap, the rode is pulled in and the boat hauled up on the anchor. To ensure that the boat is under control when the anchor breaks out, the skipper should be ready at the helm to steer it onto the required tack, and the jib sheet-hand ready to back the jib.

At the moment the anchor is aweigh (no longer hooked on the bottom), the jib is backed to the opposite side, to the required tack, which will cause the bow to swing away from the wind (see p47). If the boat is moving through the water as a result of being pulled up on the rode, the rudder can be used to assist with this manoeuvre.

As soon as the head has paid off (turned) sufficiently, the mainsail is sheeted on and the jib switched to the correct side where it is then sheeted on and the boat is sailed off. (Be careful that the crew does not get hit with either the jib or the sheet as this happens.)

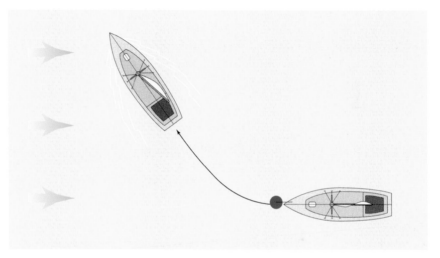

To release the anchor when the wind is ahead, first hoist the mainsail, then pull the boat forward on the cable to break out the anchor (or release the mooring by pulling it along the side of the boat) and turn the boat. Sail off.

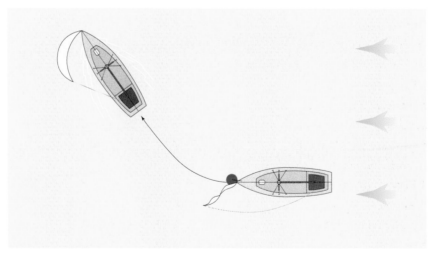

When the wind is coming from behind (aft), hoist the headsail and immediately raise the anchor (or drop the mooring). Sail well clear before hoisting the mainsail.

An electric windlass takes the strain out of weighing anchor

SAILING ONTO A JETTY

Once again, this technique uses the same basic principle as picking up a mooring buoy (see p53) but, because there is less sea room to manoeuvre, greater accuracy in handling the boat and greater skills in judging the approach are required; a jetty is a more substantial object than a buoy and mistakes can be rather costly! Also, because it is a fixed object, sailing onto a jetty requires a different approach for each change in wind direction. In all instances, fenders should be in place in case of any bumps when coming alongside.

Assuming the jetty sticks straight out from the shore, when there is either an onshore or an offshore wind, the procedure is similar to sailing up to a mooring buoy.

If the wind is offshore, the initial approach is made on a reach to seaward of the jetty at the required distance off. When off the end of the jetty, the sheets are freed and the boat is rounded up into the wind to slide alongside the jetty as the boat loses momentum.

If the wind is onshore, the boat must be taken inshore in order to gain enough manoeuvring room to round up alongside the jetty, using the same procedure.

With the wind blowing across the jetty, it becomes difficult to berth alongside under sail without considerable risk, as the final approach will head the boat directly at the jetty, and even the slightest misjudgement of speed or distance will result in a collision. If there is sufficient room across the end of the jetty, then that is the best place to aim for, with the boat approaching the jetty across-wind and then rounding up to berth at the end of the jetty. In these wind conditions, trying to berth somewhere along the length of the jetty is fraught with danger.

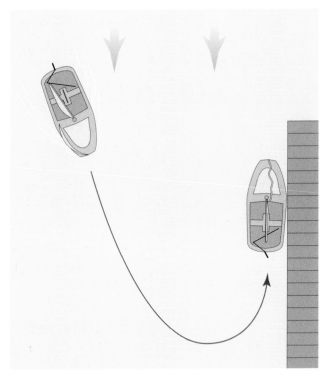

When the wind is onshore (coming from behind as you approach the shore), take the boat closer inshore in order to create manoeuvring room, then round up and come alongside the jetty.

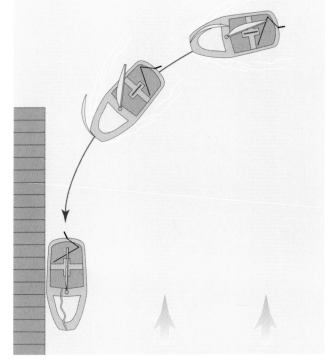

When approaching a jetty into the wind (an offshore wind), sail towards it on a reach. At the end of the jetty, free the sails to slow down the boat and round up (turn into the wind) to stop alongside the jetty. The escape route is on a reach away from the jetty.

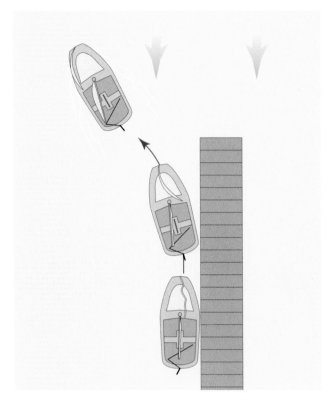

When the wind is blowing onshore, the boat may be facing into the wind. In this case, back the jib to push the bow away from the jetty. Once clear, the mainsail can be sheeted on and the jib switched to the correct side as the boat sails away.

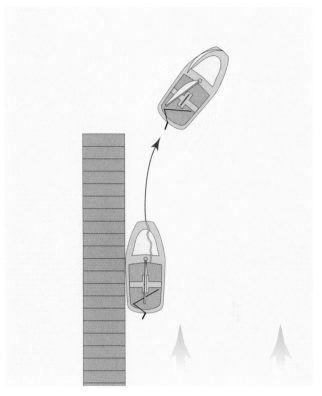

With an offshore wind (weather shore), either walk the boat to the end of the jetty, push the bow away, climb aboard and sail off on a close-haul, or hoist the jib to pull the boat to the end of the jetty, from where it can be steered clear before the mainsail is hoisted.

SAILING OFF A JETTY

Assuming the boat is lying alongside the jetty, this is a relatively easy manoeuvre except under one condition: when the wind is across the jetty and the boat is on the windward side.

If the boat is on the lee side, it is simply a matter of releasing the shore lines, letting the boat drift clear of the jetty and sheeting on the sails. But sailing off the windward side can be difficult as the boat will be pressed against the jetty by the wind and it will be hard to hoist the sails, which will probably wrap around the jetty structure.

Even if the sails can be hoisted and sheeted on to move the boat forward, it will drift to leeward at the same time and foul the jetty. The only practical way out of this problem is to hand the boat along the jetty and warp it across the end, then hoist the sails and manoeuvre out into open water.

With the wind blowing onshore, the boat will be lying alongside head to wind . The best procedure is to back the jib to push the bow away from the jetty. Once clear, the jib can be switched to the correct side, the mainsail sheeted on and the boat sailed away. The opposite situation, with the wind offshore, is even easier. The jib is hoisted to catch what will be a following wind (the mainsail may be too close to the jetty, causing the boom to snag) and sheeted on to quietly pull the boat ahead along the jetty, from where it can be steered out into the tidal stream and the mainsail can then be hoisted.

When the wind blows off the shore it is termed a weather or windward shore; when the wind blows onto the shore, it is termed a lee shore.

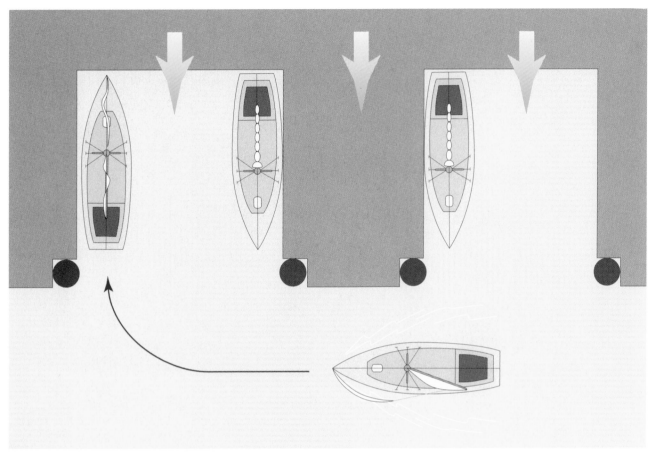

When under sail, the simplest berthing procedure is when the wind is blowing from straight ahead as you enter the berth. It is worth practising this manoeuvre first before trying to sail your boat into a marina berth in different wind (and tide) conditions.

SAILING INTO A MARINA BERTH

This tricky manoeuvre is always best carried out under power, but there may come a time when the motor is not working, or for some other reason only sail power is available. Provided there is sufficient room to manoeuvre in the often-tight confines of the marina, a competent skipper should be able to berth his boat in all but the most extreme weather conditions.

As with sailing onto a jetty, much depends on the wind direction, and sometimes basic sailing procedures must be adapted to suit the specific conditions. A competent crew standing ready with mooring lines and fenders are an essential part of this operation.

If the wind is blowing down the berth (or dock) from ahead, the routine is standard; the boat is sailed across the end of the dock, then rounded up into the wind, to slide neatly into the berth.

If the wind is across the dock, the best approach is to reduce sail to just the jib, and then sail the boat slowly into the berth, carefully reducing speed to a minimum by easing the jib and spilling wind.

When the wind is blowing onto the dock (coming from behind as you approach the berth), there are two approach options: one is to line the boat up with the berth, then free off all the sails and let the wind push the hull into the berth, a manoeuvre which requires a great deal of care and skill. The other, easier, approach is to reduce sail to just the jib and sail across the dock, slowing the boat and allowing it to drift sideways onto one arm of the dock, then handing it into position in the berth.

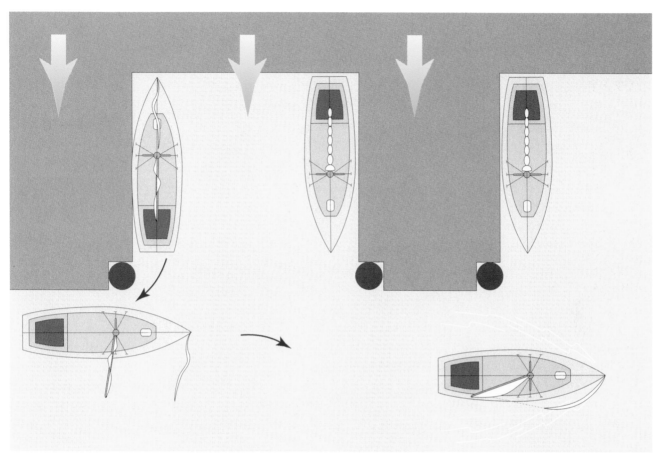

If the boat is lying head to wind in the dock, and the wind is coming from ahead, the easiest procedure is to walk the boat backwards along the berth and around the corner to the end of the dock. From here, the sheets can be taken on and the boat sailed into clear water.

SAILING OUT OF A MARINA BERTH

This is perhaps the most difficult of all berthing procedures and, once again, the success (or otherwise) of this manoeuvre will depend to a great extent on the wind direction.

If the wind is directly ahead, the sails can be hoisted and allowed to flap freely by easing the sheets right out. The boat is then physically handed backwards (pulled along by someone holding a mooring line and walking along the pontoon or jetty) out of the berth and around the corner onto the end of the dock, where the sheets are taken on and the boat sailed ahead and into clear water.

If the wind is astern as the boat lies in the marina, it will need to be handed back onto the end of the dock, this time without any sails hoisted. From here, there will be considerable difficulty getting under way because the boat will be pressed hard against the dock on the lee side. Trial and error will be the only way to get clear, as each boat will react differently.

One solution is to hoist the sails, but leave them free and flapping. Bringing the main sheet on gently, should start the boat moving and, with the assistance of someone ashore fending it off the dock, the boat may get up enough way to respond to the helm, at which point the sheets can be brought on and the boat sailed away. (Some agility may be required by the shore crew who needs to scramble aboard quickly before the boat sails out of reach!)

SAILING OFF A BEACH

Centreboard dinghies and cata-marans usually launch from a beach or ramp, so mooring and berthing techniques do not apply. Nevertheless, sailing off a beach, especially in strong onshore winds, can create problems, because a centreboard cannot be lowered in shallow water and, with no centre-board, the boat will be constantly blown back onto the beach.

There is no problem when the wind is blowing off the beach, as the centreboard is not required when running free, so the boat is simply launched with the centre-board fully retracted and sailed out into deep water. Indeed, the only danger with this exercise is that, with the wind behind it, the boat is liable to take off before the crew can jump aboard!

Much the same applies when the wind is blowing across the beach, as the centreboard need only be partly lowered in order to reach off the beach. As a rule, a boat will respond sufficiently with the centre-board in this position until it has sailed out enough to drop it fully.

Most small boats also have retractable rudders. Without being able to lower the centreboard and rudder, the boat is out of control and going nowhere in an onshore wind, except back onto the beach! However, it helps if the beach is deep close in, as a good hard push by the crew may carry it into water deep enough to lower the centre-board and rudder (see opposite).

Low tides, or launching from a beach that is naturally shallow for some way out, can be very frustrat-ing, with the boat constantly being

blown ashore before there is time to get it sailing. With experienced centreboard sailors, a favourite method is for the crew to climb aboard as soon as the boat is in the water. The sails are hoisted with sheets free to flap as the boat lies head to wind. The skipper remains in the water holding the boat and, when ready, pushes it well out, often running chest deep into the water before scrambling aboard over the transom, while the crew lowers the centreboard as far as possible and brings on the jib sheet. Once aboard, the skipper brings on the mainsheet and low-ers the rudder, by which time the boat is usually in water deep enough for the centreboard to be fully lowered, after which the boat can be sailed off.

With the bow facing out to sea, walk the boat into water deep enough for the rudder. Partially insert the centreboard.

Holding the mainsheet in one hand and the tiller in another, push the boat out and climb aboard.

Start steering a close-hauled or reaching course out to sea, sheeting the sails accordingly. Lower the centreboard and rudder once you are under way.

SAILING ONTO A BEACH

The offshore wind which makes leaving the beach so easy is the one that causes problems when coming back in. As the boat enters shallow water close to the beach, the centreboard and rudder must be retracted, at which point the boat loses momentum and is blown back off the beach.

Since a boat cannot sail directly into the wind, it cannot simply be run straight up onto the sand, but must tack in, which requires the centreboard to be fully lowered. The danger is that the centreboard will strike the bottom and break off as the boat approaches the beach, so it must be retracted fully.

With a steep beach it may be possible to keep the boat moving fast and get it close in enough so that momentum will carry it to the shore after the centreboard has been retracted. Failing that, there really is only one other way: the crew must be prepared to jump over the side the moment the centreboard is lifted and drag the boat into the beach.

If the wind is blowing onto the beach there will be no problem, as the boat will be running free and the centreboard will be retracted, so the boat can be sailed straight onto the beach.

However, with a strong wind and a fast boat, sailing straight up the beach can damage the hull. A smart, seamanlike technique is to turn the boat across the wind just

prior to hitting the beach (see below). This will cause the sails to flap (they should be run right out) while the boat drifts sideways onto the beach. The same applies if the wind is blowing across the beach, the boat runs in on a reach and at the last moment is rounded up head to wind, so it loses momentum and drifts onto the beach.

With all sailing manoeuvres, including the ones described in this chapter, much depends on the wind, the circumstances and the skills of the skipper and crew. Each boat handles differently to another and every sailing situation brings with it its own problems but, with basic knowledge and lots of practice, most sailors will soon master the handling of their own boat without too much drama.

If the wind is blowing across the shore, sail towards the beach, letting the sails right out to slow the boat.

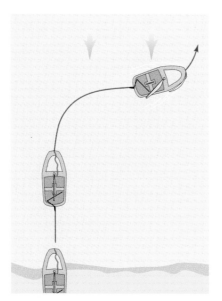

When sailing off a beach into the wind, the boat needs to be pushed out until the centreboard and rudder can be lowered.

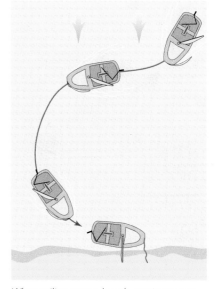

When sailing onto a beach, turning across the wind before reaching the shore reduces the risk of damaging the hull.

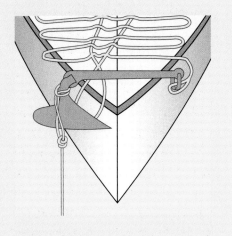  

SEAMANSHIP AND BOAT HANDLING

The term seamanship covers a multitude of activities but, essentially, it stands for the correct nautical way of doing things on a boat. Seamanship is often the result of years of experience at sea, and it cannot always be learned from a book. However, there are many basic sailing principles and actions that form the foundation of good seamanship. Some of the more common aspects of seamanship are described in this chapter, others are included in the various sailing activities and manoeuvres covered elsewhere in the book.

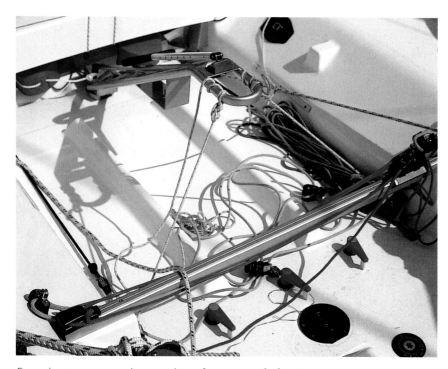

Every sheet, rope or cord on a yacht performs a specific function.

Ropes and cordage

A significant factor in seamanship is basic rope work. There are many ways to tie a knot, but there is only one correct nautical way. Sailors' lives can sometimes depend on tying or releasing a knot in a hurry and, while an ordinary knot will jam under load or when it gets wet, most sailor's knots are designed to be quickly tied and released under any conditions.

Yachts and smaller sailboats use ropes extensively. As described on p31, strong, rigid wire rope is used as standing rigging to hold the mast in place, while flexible wire rope and synthetic ropes are used for the running rigging. At the other end of the scale, fine cord is used for whipping (securing the end of a larger rope to prevent it

unravelling). In between, there are all sizes and types of synthetic ropes used for controlling the sails, mooring the boat at a dock and so on. Indeed, it would be safe to say that almost everything involved in the practical side of sailing uses a rope of some description.

Ropes can be made from many materials. Although some ropes are still made from natural fibres, these have mostly been phased out in favour of the more durable synthetic ropes which have greater strength, are kinder to the hands, and are not as vulnerable to rot. They are used mostly as halyards (for hoisting sails and sheets) and for controlling the sails.

Larger yachts may use flexible wire rope for halyards and even for some sheets and braces but on

the average family yacht, synthetic ropes are more popular.

Synthetic ropes are usually made from polypropylene, polyester or nylon. The polyesters, commonly known as Terylene and Dacron, are the most popular for everyday use. Polypropylene is mainly confined to rougher uses, such as mooring or towing lines, as it is coarser and may deteriorate in sunlight. Nylon was the first synthetic material to be used for ropes. However, its stretch factor often inhibits its use for high-load purposes, especially setting the sails, although it is widely used for towing and anchor warps, where the stretch factor can be advantageous. Nylon stretches to 45 per cent of its length, while polyester stretches to around 25 per cent of its length.

Most ropes are constructed in one of two forms: laid or braided. Laid rope is the traditional form, in which a number of strands, usually three, are twisted together; this is often called hawser laid rope and is popular with amateur sailors as it is strong and can be easily spliced.

Braided rope is woven or plaited in a number of ways, the most popular being the composite form in which an inner core of strands is enclosed within a braided (plaited) sheath. This is probably the most popular for sailboat use as it has excellent strength and is much softer on the hands than laid rope. However, because of its complex structure, it is difficult to splice.

Knots, bends and splices

Sailor's knots and bends come in many shapes and forms, with many uses. Most boats use a mix of both in the course of their sailing activities, adopting whichever is most suitable for the job in hand.

Safety is a prime factor in using sailor's knots as opposed to any others. If a sailing dinghy capsizes, putting its crew in danger, the difference between a jammed knot and one that can be released under pressure could mean the difference between a quick recovery and a catastrophe. Similarly, a crewman working at the top of a mast wants to know with certainty that the knot securing him aloft is not likely to slip, even if the rope is wet.

Splices are more secure than knots, but their use is limited to joining together two pieces of rope, or creating a permanent eye in the end of a rope.

Mooring ropes are a typical example of the use of a splice in preference to a knot. They require an eye in the end which can be dropped over bollards or cleats on a dock. The eye can be made by bending a bowline in the end of the rope but, because knots and bends are designed to free easily, such a knot can work loose with the constant surging of the boat against the dock. By contrast, an eye created with an eye splice will not shake loose. As a general rule, laid synthetic rope is used for most splicing activities.

Bowline – used to make a loop in the end of a rope, or to tie a line to a ring or post. It cannot be untied under load.

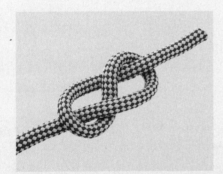

Figure of eight – a stopper knot used to prevent the end of a rope from running through a block. Easy to untie, even when wet or under load.

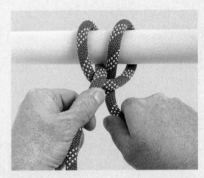

Clove hitch – used for hitching fenders to a rail, or for mooring a boat temporarily to a ring or post.

Reef knot – used for tying two ropes of equal diameter. Most commonly used when putting in a reef, hence the name.

Double sheet bend – one of the best ways of joining two ropes of unequal diameter.

Round turn and two half- hitches – often used to tie a rope to a rail or spar, as it can be tied quickly and is easy to untie.

The use of blocks on this dinghy reduces the amount of physical effort required to pull in the mainsheet.

Blocks and tackles

Tackles, incorporating a number of blocks, are more commonly known ashore as pulleys. A rope threaded through two or more separate blocks forms a labour-saving device which enables even heavy weights to be lifted with relative ease.

Blocks are made from a number of different materials, synthetics or metal being the most popular. The grooved sheaves inside the block, over which the rope is threaded, may also be made of either metal or synthetic material.

The number of sheaves in the tackle dictate how much it assists with the workload. Most main sheets have a block and tackle

system secured to the underside of the boom, usually in or near the cockpit, to make it easier to handle the mainsail. Even a moderately sized mainsail can be heavy when it is filled with wind, so a tackle is needed to relieve the weight when sailing in stiff breezes.

Jibs do not usually have tackles because they would be too cumbersome, and could bang around the rigging and deck when in use. Jib sheets are usually tensioned with sheet winches located on either side of the cockpit.

The number of blocks used in the tackle dictates the amount by which the load is reduced. This is known as its mechanical advantage (MA),

and is calculated by the number of ropes at the moving block. For example, the simplest tackle, with a single sheave used to pull down and tension the luff of a sail, would have one end of the rope attached to the deck, and the rope running up through the block and down to the person pulling on the other end. The mechanical advantage here is two. A tackle with a double block secured at the top and a single at the bottom, secured to the deck, has a MA of three, increasing the normal pulling power by three.

A small portable tackle called a 'handy billy' is often kept aboard to facilitate any work that might require a bit of extra muscle.

Tying a heaving line knot

This knot can be quickly formed and is readily undone. To make a heaving line, use a doubled bight and complete the same steps as below, tucking the working end through both parts of the bight, keeping the wraps tight. If you are trying to get a heavy hawser to the shore, use a sheet bend to haul the heavier line (see p66). The alternative name for this knot, a Franciscan knot, probably comes from its similarity to the tassel-like girdle on the traditional monk's habit.

Form a bight in the end of your sheet, about 60cm (24in) long, depending on its thickness. About 25cm (10in) from the bight, start wrapping the working end around the parts of the bight. Work toward the end of the bight and make your first pass lock down over itself.

Continue making turns around the parts of the bight until you have used up all the line. Be sure that each wrap is tightened as you go, to ensure maximum density in the finished knot.

Tuck the working end through the last visible part of the bight, then pull down on the standing part to tighten the bight onto the working end. Voilà! Your knot is completed.

Heaving lines

One of the most commonly used ropes, on boats of any size, is the heaving line. This is a light line for throwing to another boat in order to pass a towing line, or to someone on the dock to send ashore mooring lines, or whenever contact across a gap is required.

Once the heaving line has been received, the heavier towing or mooring lines are attached to it and pulled across the intervening water. Although light in weight, it should be strong and of sufficient length to cover a fair distance.

Throwing a heaving line is an art that is lacking in most amateur sailors today, but it is considered an important part of the skills of professional seamen, as it is frequently a very useful attribute.

The throwing end of the line is first secured to a modest weight, often a decorative knot known as a 'Monkey's Fist'. The line is then coiled up in a clockwise direction in the left hand (assuming the thrower to be right-handed) and, when coiled, it is carefully divided into two sections, with the larger amount in the left hand. The rope in the right hand (with the weight or 'Monkey's Fist' at the end) is swung back and thrown, while the left hand is opened to allow the remainder of the coil to run out. The purpose of this technique is firstly to reduce the weight of the line for throwing, thus gaining more distance, and secondly, to reduce the risk of the rope tangling during the throw.

Because a throwing line is sometimes required in an emergency situation, at least one of the crew should be skilled in the technique.

Boat handling under power

However much purists may disparage the use of motors in sailboats there comes a time in every skipper's life when he thanks his lucky stars for the engine fitted below decks. Many a boat has been rescued from a watery grave and, equally important, many a man overboard has lived to tell the tale, because the motor kicked into life at a critical moment. So, regardless of the aesthetics, a motor is an important part of a boat's safety equipment; a fact which even authorities in the pristine world of performance yacht racing have recognized in recent years.

Fitting a motor is one thing, and there are marine motors to suit all types of boats, but handling a boat under power is another. Unlike a car, which has brakes and is not much affected by outside conditions, a boat has no brakes and can be affected considerably by outside factors such as wind and tide. Knowing how to handle a boat while under power can avoid a lot of embarrassment, perhaps danger, and certainly costly repairs.

When a boat's motor is put into forward gear, the boat does not move straight ahead, as does a car. Instead, the torque of the propeller (also called the propeller side effect, or prop walk), causes the bow to swing one way or the other, depending on whether the propeller rotates in a right-hand (clockwise) or left-hand (anti-clockwise) direction. This effect can be quite considerable, catching an uninitiated boat handler by surprise.

For example, if the boat is moving alongside a berth or jetty and the motor is revved up in reverse, the bow will suddenly swing to starboard (in the case of a right-handed propeller) and could cause the boat to collide with the berth. Although the rudder can sometimes help to avoid such situations, with the motor going astern the rudder is often ineffective and cannot be relied on.

It is important to get to know how a boat reacts to the motor before using it in tight confines, such as a marina dock. Take the boat out into clear water and practise powering ahead and astern from a stationary position to learn which way the bow swings, and by how much.

If the propeller is right-handed (it turns clockwise when viewed from astern) the torque (propeller side effect) will swing the boat's bow to port when going ahead and to starboard when going astern. A left-handed propeller will have the opposite effect.

When taking over the helm of a strange boat, if you are in doubt as to whether a propeller is left- or right-handed, this exercise will soon indicate which it is by the way in which the bow swings.

Another thing to remember when using the motor is that the rudder requires a flow of water across its

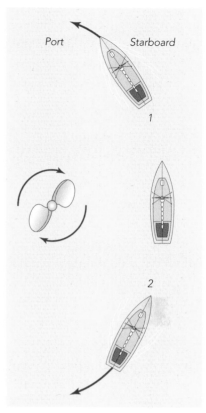

An engine with a right-hand (clockwise) rotating propeller will cause the bow to swing to port when going ahead (1). When going astern (in reverse), the opposite occurs. with the bow swinging to starboard and the stern to port (2).

surface to make it effective. When the motor is going ahead, the propeller sends a surge of water across the rudder blade (mostly astern of the propeller) which creates good steering response. When going astern, the thrust of the propeller directs the flow of water forward and thus away from the rudder, so steering response will be poor. Only when the boat gathers speed astern will the normal flow of water enable the rudder to respond.

Berthing under power

Since most problems that occur with handling a boat under power arise when berthing ('parking' a boat), the following offers some guidance on the methods used under differing conditions to put a boat alongside a marina berth or jetty. The descriptions are all for right-handed propellers (see p69).

WIND AHEAD OR ASTERN

If the wind is ahead much depends on which side the dock lies. If it is on the port side, the boat can be angled in slightly until the bow is in position and secured against the berth, then a short burst astern on the motor will draw the stern alongside. The approach is much the same when berthing starboard side to. With the bow placed alongside and secured, a brief burst ahead on the motor with the helm hard over to port, will push the stern alongside the berth.

With the wind coming from behind, the same procedures can be followed. However, since more reverse power will be required to hold the boat against the wind, care must be taken to anticipate the increased torque effect.

WIND BLOWING ONTO THE BERTH

The best approach is to let the wind do the work. Take the boat into the dock slowly until it is level with the berth but with the bow slightly angled into the wind and about one metre or so off, then

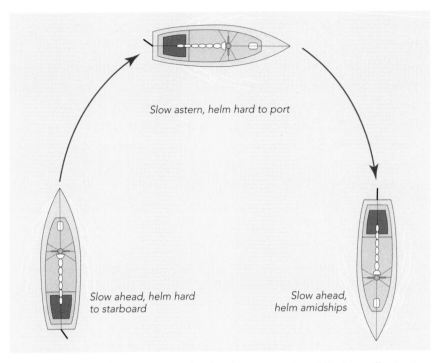

Slow astern, helm hard to port

Slow ahead, helm hard to starboard

Slow ahead, helm amidships

To turn a boat in a tight space, motor ahead and steer to starboard (the bow will swing to starboard). Reverse the motor, so the prop walk (torque) pushes the stern to port, as the bow continues to swing to starboard (right-handed prop). Repeat the actions until the boat has turned 180 degrees. With this technique, some boats can turn within their own length.

reverse the motor gently to avoid any torque effect. When the boat stops, it should blow gently onto the berth, the angled bow falling off first so that it should be aligned when the boat comes alongside.

WIND BLOWING OFF THE BERTH (STARBOARD SIDE TO)

This is trickier because the boat will blow away from the berth when stopped. The use of the torque effect can help here. Take the boat into the berth as close as possible, throw a stern line ashore and secure it. Reverse the motor quite firmly. With the stern secured, the torque of the propeller will draw the bow into the berth against the wind. It is

important to get the bowline on as quickly as possible, before the wind blows it away from the berth.

WIND OFF THE BERTH (PORT SIDE TO)

Here, the torque is used to achieve a different effect. Head the boat into the berth at a slight angle and get a line ashore from the bow as soon as possible, then pull the bow close to the berth and secure the line. Put the motor ahead and the helm hard to starboard and the combined effect of propeller and rudder will push the stern into the berth and place the boat snugly alongside. Reversing the motor when the bow is secured to the dock can have the same effect.

Anchoring and mooring

Apart from being handy for everyday use, an anchor is a vital part of a boat's safety equipment, something not always appreciated by boat owners. When all else fails, the anchor is often the one piece of equipment that can save a boat in an emergency.

Dismasting, or engine failure close to a lee shore, are typical examples of how using an anchor can mean the difference between safety and disaster. The anchor is an inexpensive, simple, piece of equipment, but having one aboard can pay dividends a thousand times over in a crisis.

Basically, an anchor is designed to hold a boat in position, such as for a pleasant family picnic in a sheltered bay, or while the crew go ashore to enjoy the offerings of a new harbour.

Provided the anchor is right for the boat, and the holding ground (the underwater surface into which an anchor grips) is good, it will provide security under most conditions, keeping the boat in position, head to wind or head to tide, whichever is stronger, with no stress on either the boat or crew.

TYPES OF ANCHOR

There are many different types of anchor and using the correct type is important because, if it is to hold securely, it must dig firmly into the sea bed. An anchor which holds well in sand may not get a grip on smooth rock, while one designed to hold on rocky reefs may not dig into a sandy or muddy bottom. Similarly, an anchor that is too light for the boat will bounce across the sea bed or pull out as soon as any weight comes on it; while one that is too heavy will snag easily on almost anything and ensure that the crew suffer hernias when pulling it up! Ship chandlers will advise on the correct weight of anchor for a specific boat, while the type or design will depend on its intended use.

For general use on keel yachts, the most common anchors are the Danforth, Plough (CQR), Bruce and the Admiralty (fisherman type).

The Danforth is probably the most widely used as it offers easy stowage and a reasonable grip on most soft sea beds. The Plough, or CQR, is particularly good for sandy or muddy bottoms, but it may not hold on rocky reefs. The one-piece casting of the Bruce gives it great strength and good holding in rocky ground, as well as sand and mud. These types of anchor are normally permanently fitted to the bow of larger boats.

When it comes to good holding, in weed or rock, the best anchor is the traditionally shaped Admiralty type. Once firmly dug into the sea bottom, it will almost never drag. However, as it is both heavy, and cumbersome to stow, it is not popular on yachts, where space is often at a premium.

Danforth anchor

Plough (CQR) anchor

Bruce anchor

Grapnels, or reef anchors, have a structure that is similar to an umbrella, where the 'ribs' catch in the rocky crevices of reefs, but they are quite useless on sand or mud. Grapnels are difficult to stow, but folding versions are popular, especially on dinghies.

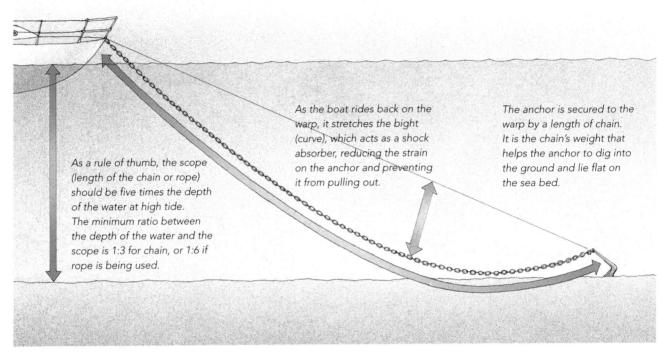

As a rule of thumb, the scope (length of the chain or rope) should be five times the depth of the water at high tide. The minimum ratio between the depth of the water and the scope is 1:3 for chain, or 1:6 if rope is being used.

As the boat rides back on the warp, it stretches the bight (curve), which acts as a shock absorber, reducing the strain on the anchor and preventing it from pulling out.

The anchor is secured to the warp by a length of chain. It is the chain's weight that helps the anchor to dig into the ground and lie flat on the sea bed.

An anchor needs to lie flat on the sea bed and it can only do this if the warp hangs in a curve (or bight). The longer the warp, the better the anchor holds, so let out more chain or rope if the wind gains strength or the sea gets too rough.

THE WARP OR RODE

An important factor for secure anchoring is the warp or rode (cable or line) which is shackled to the anchor before use. The warp absorbs much of the strain on the anchor, preventing it from pulling out of the sea bed as the boat rides back on it. A sudden surge, or excessive pull on the anchor, will pluck it from the bottom, so the warp is designed to absorb surge and hold the anchor in position.

This is achieved in one of two ways; firstly the length of the warp paid out must be considerably more than the depth of the water, thus allowing it to hang in a bight (curve). Five times the depth of water is a good length for a secure anchorage in normal conditions, although for casual anchoring in well sheltered water, a shorter warp may be used. As the boat rides back on the warp it stretches the bight. This acts as a shock absorber, reducing the strain on the anchor and preventing it from pulling out. It is a basic maxim of safe anchoring that the longer the warp, the better the anchor holds, so if the wind gets up or things do not appear to be comfortable, more warp must be let out.

Secondly, the anchor is secured to the warp by a length of chain. This increases the shock absorbing effect of the bight and helps drive the anchor flukes deeper into the sea bed. The chain's weight causes it to lie along the bottom and thus reduce the angle at which the warp pulls on the anchor. The best holding position of any anchor is with the shank lying flat along the sea bed because this drives the flukes deeper into the bottom.

A good length of fairly heavy chain plus a long warp are the remedy for getting an undisturbed night's sleep when at anchor.

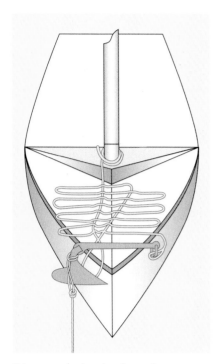

Prior to anchoring, lay the anchor across the bow as shown, with the anchor warp tied to the mast and flaked.

THE ANCHORING PROCEDURE

There are a number of ways to drop anchor successfully, although the most practical method is with the boat lying head to wind, since this is the position it will adopt when the anchor takes up.

The procedure for anchoring under sail is given on p56, but using the motor is probably easier, and safer, especially in crowded anchorages. Going astern on the motor, instead of just drifting back on the warp, offers more control, and drives the anchor more firmly into the sea bed. When the anchor digs in, the warp will tighten and the boat will come up head to wind, after which the motor can be switched off.

The anchor chain is prepared and laid ready on deck prior to the anchor being paid out.

WEIGHING ANCHOR

Weighing anchor when using the motor simply involves motoring ahead while taking in the warp until the anchor is directly under the boat, at which point it should just pluck out of the sea bed. If it becomes fouled and cannot be pulled out by hand, greater pressure can be applied by securing the warp to the forward bollard or cleat and motoring ahead over the anchor. This will reverse the angle of the warp and should pluck the anchor out without too much effort. Some anchors have a tripping line secured to the flukes, which works in much the same way, by plucking the anchor out backwards.

Weighing anchor under sail is a basic sailing manoeuvre (see p57).

THE ANCHORAGE POSITION

It is unwise to leave a boat at anchor without someone aboard, for, no matter how secure the anchorage, a boat can easily drag anchor and find itself in trouble before any alarm is raised. Much the same applies when sleeping on board; the boat's position should be checked at least once during the night, more often if weather conditions deteriorate, to ensure it is not dragging anchor.

Indeed, even during daylight hours, a wise skipper will keep an eye on the shore for any sign that the anchor is not secure. When the boat is first established on the anchoring position, a check should be made on its location and marked on the chart. At any sign of the anchor dragging, a quick look at the chart will confirm it.

The charted position should be established with compass readings for a cross bearing fix (see p125). GPS can be used, although it might be difficult to pinpoint your exact position if the anchorage is tight and crowded.

Once the anchorage position has been established and a transit bearing of two shore objects has been aligned and plotted, the boat's position can be checked visually without the need for a GPS, compass, or even the chart, but simply by using transit bearings.

A transit bearing is one which aligns the boat with two prominent objects, preferably one closer and

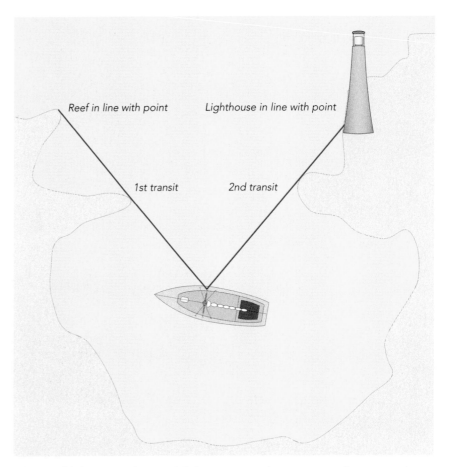

When establishing an anchorage, it is important to take compass readings or transit bearings on shore objects so that you have a reference point in case the anchor drags.

lower and the other distant and higher (as depicted in the illustration). If the two objects move out of alignment, it is likely the boat is dragging anchor.

A more accurate check can be made by establishing a second set of transits at roughly 90 degrees to the first. Then, no matter which way the boat drags, one of the two transits will indicate it.

The anchor may drag as a result of a number of factors, the most common being that it was not set correctly in the first place. If the warp is too short or the flukes of

the anchor are fouled with weed or with its own chain, the anchor will not dig into the sea bed and the boat will drag astern. In this case the anchor must be raised and cleared before being reset. In most other cases, letting out more anchor warp will generally overcome the problem.

For long-term anchoring, there are various procedures for dropping two separate anchors but, as these require considerable seamanship skills, especially when carried out under sail, they are rarely used in normal sailing.

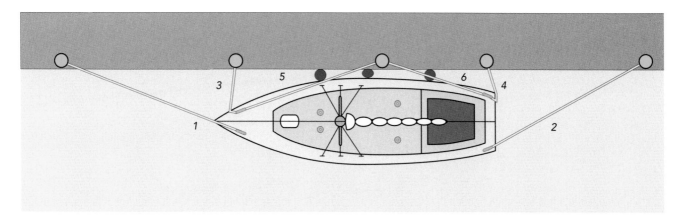

*Above: The main mooring ropes (warps).
Use what is necessary to hold the boat
under the prevailing conditions.*

1) Bow line   2) Stern line
3) Fore breast rope   4) Aft breast rope
5) Fore spring   6) Aft spring

*Right: Depending which side of a jetty
you tie up to, you may need to use
fenders to counter the effects of the
wind and/or tide pushing the hull against
the dock.*

Tying up to a dock

Marina berths (pens) in sheltered harbours do not usually experience a great deal of movement in the water, so tying up is a simple process, and most marinas provide mooring lines already attached to the dock or pontoons.

Jetties and wharves in more open spaces are often subject to tides, wave surges as a result of passing ship or ferry traffic, or are exposed to wind directions from a certain quarter. To ensure the boat is secure at all times, especially when no-one is aboard, it should be tied up so as to counter anything which might try to dislodge it.

For complete security, the full system of mooring ropes (see above) can be used but, as a general rule, you only need those that are essential for the prevailing conditions.

Bow and stern lines are necessary, as these prevent forward and backward movement, but tend to allow the boat to move in and out from the wharf a little.

Fenders can be used to avoid any damage to the hull, but it is usually better to snug the boat comfortably alongside. For this, breast ropes should be run from near the bow and stern, roughly at right angles to the centre line of the boat, to prevent sideways movement.

Where conditions are likely to be bad, for instance where the boat may surge strongly along the wharf, as happens in harbours open to the ocean swell, spring lines are normally used to prevent excessive backward and forward movement. The fore spring runs for about one third of the length of the boat, from the bow to a point (bollard or cleat) on the dock fairly well aft, while the aft spring runs from a point at the stern to a point well forward on the dock. When used in conjunction with the other lines, the springs help to hold the boat in place in all except the strongest winds.

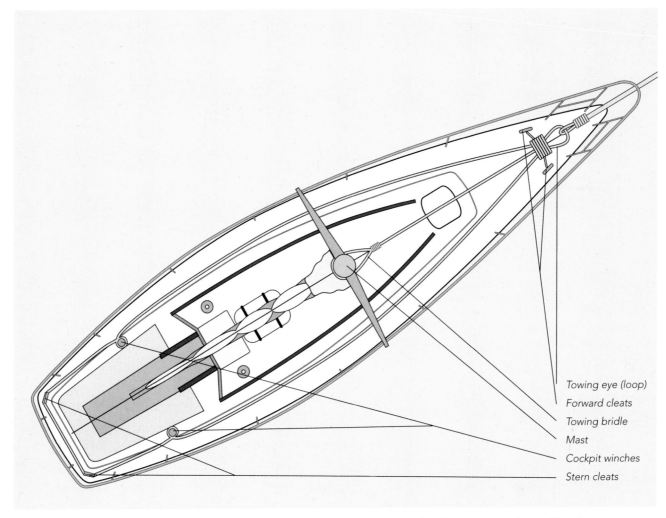

Towing eye (loop)
Forward cleats
Towing bridle
Mast
Cockpit winches
Stern cleats

The majority of yachts do not have cleats strong enough to cope with the load associated with towing in rough seas. Therefore a towing bridle is attached to the mast, and warps are led around two winches with the towing eye on the foredeck 60cm (2ft) aft of the bow.

Taking on a tow

At some stage, most boats will need to be towed or to tow someone else. In good conditions, this is a simple process, involving passing a tow line and proceeding under power at a moderate speed.

But, when the wind is strong and the sea is rough, this can become a real test of seamanship. Getting a tow line aboard can be hazardous in difficult conditions, as getting close enough to throw a heaving line means the towing boat must manoeuvre close to the stricken vessel, at the risk of colliding with it. This is when the skill of throwing a heaving line (see p68), as well as competent boat handling, can affect the outcome. The further the heaving line can be thrown, the greater the distance that can be maintained. A crewman with good throwing skills will enable the two boats to stay far enough apart to avoid a collision.

When the heaving line lands on the tow, the towing line can be attached to it and passed across, before being secured to adequate fittings on the bow of the vessel being towed.

The fittings on dinghies are usually fairly light and can easily be pulled out while towing, so the tow line should be passed through an eye or cleat on the bow and secured around the base of the mast or a forward thwart.

A flotilla of dinghies is towed out of a marina to begin the day's sailing in clear waters. Even when towing under these controlled conditions, it is important to observe the correct following procedures.

The towing boat then gradually takes up the strain until the boat being towed responds and begins to follow. Unless it is impossible for safety reasons, it is important that the towed boat is steered to follow the towing boat, to reduce the strain caused by the towed boat yawing (rolling) from side to side.

For open sea towing, the tow line should be long; whereas in harbours or congested areas it should be shortened to keep the tow under control. Some skippers even favour securing the tow alongside in tight situations.

Centreboard dinghies and small boats often need to be towed when they have been capsized or swamped. When this occurs, they must first be righted and their sails taken down, or they are liable to get out of control and may capsize again while under tow. If the boat has been dismasted, the towing boat must take care not to get entangled in sails or rigging in the water when passing the tow line. A flooded boat is very heavy and unstable and may need to be bailed out before the tow can proceed.

Centreboarders do not usually sail in open water, so towing conditions should be less hazardous than in a seaway, but caution must be exercised when manoeuvring a towed boat through a crowded marina or anchorage.

Rules of the road

The International Regulations for Preventing Collisions at Sea (IRPCS, generally known as the Colregs) apply to commercial and leisure vessels in all navigable waters around the world, unless local rules apply.

The Colregs are far too complex and detailed to be described in full and, in any case, many are aimed at commercial shipping rather than at recreational or leisure sailing. The rules included here have been selected for their application to small craft, particularly cruising yachts, but also centreboarders and catamarans. Racing yachts have their own rules, which are also based on the Colregs (see p158).

The basic Colregs require that:

1. Every vessel must maintain a proper lookout at all times. (This is particularly important for sailboats that carry a large headsail; someone should be stationed on the lee side to keep a lookout under the jib.)

2. Every vessel must at all times proceed at a safe speed. (Although this applies more to power boats, some fast catamarans and large keel yachts travel at quite high speeds and need to take care in confined waters where smaller sailboats may be operating.)

3. A vessel must use all available means to determine if risk of collision with another vessel exists. One way of doing this is to align an approaching boat on a transit bearing with some part of your boat (e.g. a shroud). If the bearing does not change, a risk of collision exists. A compass bearing can also be used.

4. Any action taken to avoid collision must be positive and made in good time. (Leaving it to the last moment can confuse the other boat; a wide sweep under his stern or a tack away from his course is the best action for sailboats.)

5. Powerboats give way to sailboats, but certain commercial vessels, such as fishing boats, ferries and large ocean-going ships, have right of way over all leisure craft when in harbours and estuaries. (The Sailing Directions for each port or harbour will indicate which vessels have right of way.)

6. When in narrow channels, keep to the starboard side of the channel (pass port to port).

7. When two sailing vessels are closing on different tacks, the boat on the port tack must give way to the boat on the starboard tack.

8. When two boats have the wind on the same side, the boat which has the wind first (windward boat) must keep clear of the other. (This is logical since the windward boat will blanket the other and leave it with no wind to manoeuvre.)

9. Any vessel overtaking another must keep clear of the boat being overtaken. (This applies even in the unlikely case of a small yacht overtaking a power boat!)

10. The boat which has right of way must maintain its course and speed. (However, this rule is qualified by stating that if the giving-way boat gets too close for safety, the right-of-way boat must take avoiding action.)

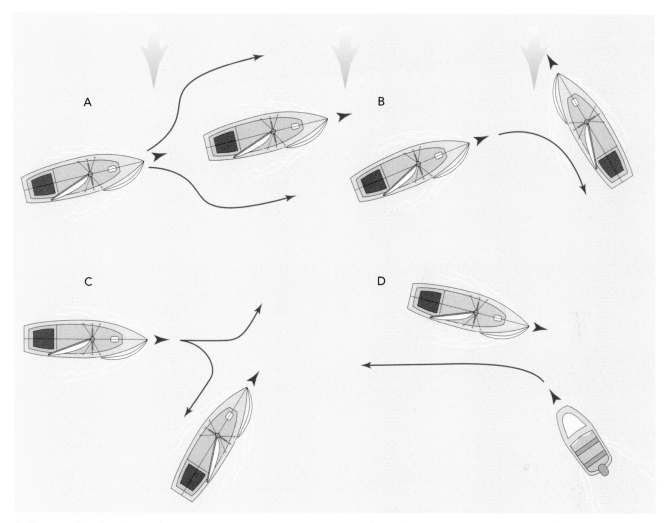

A *The overtaking boat keeps clear.*
B *A boat on port tack gives way to one on starboard tack.*

C *The windward boat keeps clear.*
D *A boat under power gives way to a sail boat.*

In racing conditions, special rules may apply.

Here, the overtaking boat must keep clear of the boat ahead.

Lights

Every sailboat is required to carry lights at night, depending on whether it is under sail or power. Sailboat skippers should know the lights of other vessels so that at night each vessel knows what the other is doing. The principal lights required by the regulations are depicted here.

1. Side lights: Starboard = green; Port = red. Stern = white light. Steaming light (used only when under power) = white light forward of the mast.

Illustrations 2–7 show the same situation from the side and the top.

2. Small boats (>7m/23ft), capable of less than seven knots, can carry an all-round white light in lieu of other lights.

3. Small boats under power: side, stern and steaming lights.

4. Boats of 7–20m (23–65½ft) under sail: side and stern lights.

5. Boats of 7–20m (23–65½ft) under power: side, stern and steaming lights. (Optional to have combined or separate port/starboard lights.)

6. Boats of 7–20m (23– 65½ft) have the option of a tricolour on the masthead when under sail.

7. Below 12m (39ft) under power: side lights and all-round masthead light (or side, steaming and stern lights).

8. Power-driven (>50m/164ft).

9. Pilot vessel: white over red light.

10. A power vessel under way carries stern and side lights, plus two white masthead lights, the front one lower than the rear.

11. Vessels under 50m (164ft) at anchor must show an all-round white light. In many waterways, this applies to all boats at anchor.

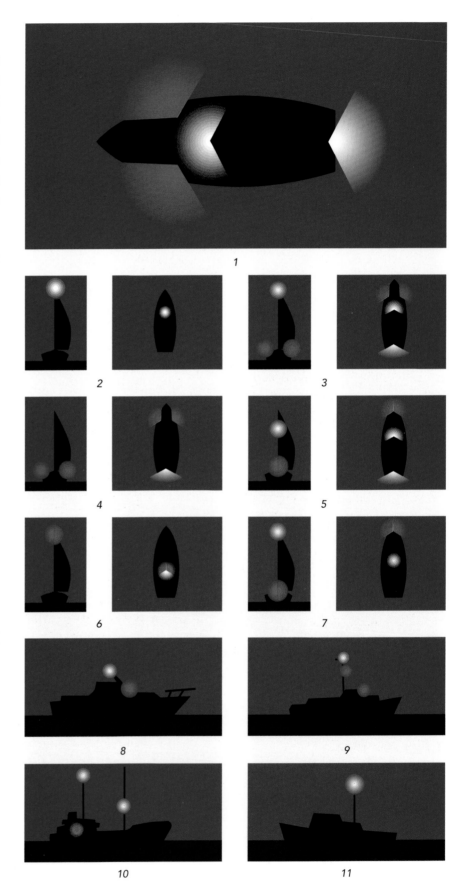

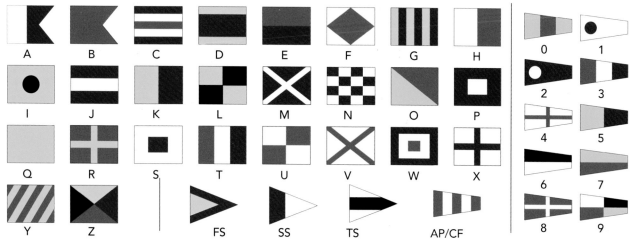

A B C D E F G H

0 1

I J K L M N O P

2 3

4 5

Q R S T U V W X

6 7

Y Z FS SS TS AP/CF

8 9

Maritime code flags

Although signal flags are no longer used to spell out long messages, they still play a valuable communications role. The A flag, for instance, indicates that a diver is in the water; while the yellow Q flag, which is flown from the starboard spreader when entering a port for the first time, shows that everyone on board is healthy and requests inward clearance from the port health authorities.

Under the International Code of Signals, the following applies:

A (Alpha)   Diver down; keep clear and
               pass at low speed.
B (Bravo)   Loading, unloading or
               carrying dangerous goods.
C (Charlie)   Yes; confirmation of
               preceding signal.
D (Delta)   Keep clear, I am
               manoeuvring with difficulty.
E (Echo)   Altering course to starboard.
F (Foxtrot)   Communicate with me.
G (Golf)   I require a pilot.
               (On a fishing vessel this
               means: I am hauling in nets).
H (Hotel)   I have a pilot on board.
I (India)   Altering course to port.
J (Juliet)   On fire and have dangerous
               cargo on board; keep clear.

K (Kilo)   I wish to communicate with you.
L (Lima)   Stop your vessel immediately.
M (Mike)   My vessel is stopped and is
               making no way through the
               water.
N (November)   No (the preceding signal
               should be read in the
               negative).
O (Oscar)   Man overboard.
P (Papa)   About to put to sea.
Q (Quebec)   My vessel is healthy and
               I request clearance to
               come ashore.
R (Romeo)   Single letter code R has no
               allocated meaning; see the
               IRPCS (Colregs).
S (Sierra)   Going astern under power.
T (Tango)   Keep clear; engaged in
               pair trawling.
U (Uniform)   You are running into danger.
V (Victor)   Assistance required.
W (Whisky)   Medical assistance required.
X (X-ray)   Stop carrying out your
               intentions and watch for
               my signals.
Y (Yankee)   Dragging anchor.
Z (Zulu)   I require a tug. (On a fishing
               vessel: I am shooting nets).
FS   First substitute.
SS   Second substitute.
TS   Third substitute.
AP + CF   (Answering pennant and
               code flag). Flown to show
               that the international code
               flags are being used, and to
               acknowledge a message.
0 (zero) to 9 Numerals.

Shapes

Shapes are designed to indicate what a vessel is doing or intending to do, although most are confined to commercial vessels and only a few apply to yachts. The only shape generally exhibited by small craft is a black ball hung forward to indicate the boat is anchored, although, strictly speaking, a vessel under both power and sail should exhibit an inverted cone.

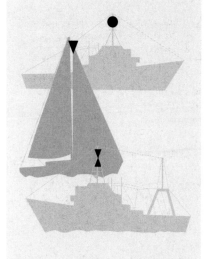

Vessel at anchor (top), under power and sail (centre); fishing or trawling (bottom).

HANDLING EMERGENCIES

Because sailboats are directly affected by the elements, they are more vulnerable to hazardous situations than most other craft. This is particularly the case with yachts which put out into the open sea, where conditions can deteriorate quickly and help is not always immediately to hand. Although problems can arise in the sheltered waters of harbours and estuaries, they are rarely as serious as those that occur in open seas.

'Be Prepared' is a good basic maxim for sailors, for the difference between disaster and survival at sea can often depend on how well prepared the boat and crew are for any eventuality. The first, and most obvious, step is to ensure that the boat is sound, seaworthy and correctly designed for the waters in which it is to sail, and that the crew members are briefed in how to use all the emergency equipment.

Small boats can sail safely on lakes and sheltered inland waters, but must be prepared to deal with sudden wind shifts, choppy waves or even squalls brought about by local weather conditions, especially if the lake is surrounded by high ground.

A safe boat

Dinghies or small yachts without self-draining cockpits should never sail in offshore waters. Without a self-draining cockpit, there is no way to get rid of the water if waves board the boat, and it will soon be swamped and will probably sink.

Survival will involve hanging onto a foundering boat in a seaway, hoping that someone will come to the rescue, for small boats seldom carry life rafts or other sea-going survival gear.

While conditions may vary from place to place, and also from waterway to waterway, a broad assessment of the type of craft best suited to sailing in different waters under normal weather conditions and with a competent skipper aboard is as follows:

Sheltered lakes, bays, harbours and estuaries where the shore is close at hand: Most types of boats can sail in these waters, but small, open boats must be fitted with buoyancy, for squally winds can quickly whip up nasty seas in the shallow water, which may swamp or capsize them. With buoyancy to keep the boat afloat, and the crew wearing life jackets, they may be able to bail out the boat and get moving again. At worst they can sit in the boat or hang onto it until rescuers arrive.

Wide lakes, bays and estuaries with a long fetch (an open area across which the wind blows with nothing to break it): Centreboard dinghies and catamarans must be fitted with buoyancy and should take care if venturing far out, but

larger boats with buoyancy or self-draining capabilities, and all yachts with ballast keels, can sail on these waters, bearing in mind the hazards that can arise with shallow water and strong tidal flows.

Exposed coastal waters: Unless designed for offshore, no centreboard dinghy or catamaran should take to the open sea. Small yachts with self-draining cockpits and a ballast keel will be fine, providing they have the necessary offshore safety gear including a radio, EPIRB (see p85), and life raft.

Open ocean: Large keel yachts equipped with offshore safety gear, including INMARSAT and GPS, are the only sailing vessels which can attempt to sail across open oceans or venture any distance from sheltered coastal waters.

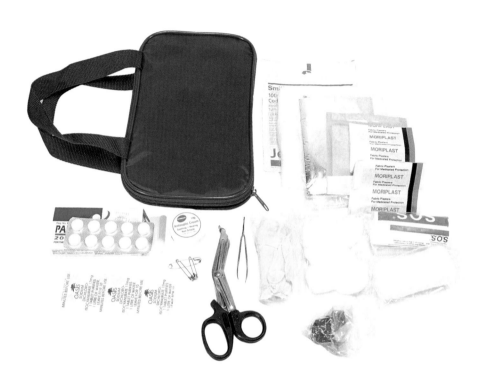

It is worth investing in a decent first aid kit and replenishing it whenever anything is used. Even small cuts or abrasions are easier to cope with if you have the right items to hand.

a motor, a galley or other features with a high fire risk, but they are rarely part of the equipment on sailing dinghies or other small boats without motors. It is important to use the correct type of extinguisher on a yacht because of the confined accommodation space inside the hull. Using carbon dioxide extinguishers in the cabin would probably put out the operator before the fire. Dry powder (chemical) fire-extinguishers are best suited for on-board use, but fire blankets, sand or any other smothering medium can be used.

Man overboard

Although this is one of the most scary emergencies at sea, it generally is not a problem if weather conditions are favourable and the boat is fitted with a motor.

A 'man overboard' button electronically keeps track of the man overboard's position on the GPS/chart plotter and enables the boat to return to that position; a useful feature in a high swell or poor visibility when the lookout may lose sight of him. It must be pressed the moment the alarm is sounded,

Once the alarm is raised, the motor is started, the sails dropped and the boat swung round to a position downwind of the person in the water. By approaching into the wind at a slow speed, the boat can be kept under full control until it is alongside the person, who is then swung aboard.

Fire-extinguishers must be serviced annually by an approved contractor.

First aid kit: As essential at sea as it is anywhere on shore. The contents of the first-aid kit should be appropriate for the type of sailing being undertaken, bearing in mind that doctors are not usually available in the middle of an ocean. It is important to check the contents at least once a year, replacing any items that are out of date. Always replenish the kit before undertaking a long voyage.

Fire-extinguisher: Once again, a safety item that is as important ashore as it is at sea. Yachts must carry fire-extinguishers if they have

The pick-up should be made on the lee side, so the wind does not blow the boat away from the person in the water. Calmer water on the lee side also makes it easier to lift the person aboard. (It is also possible to make the pick-up on the weather, or windward, side.)

Take care to ensure that the person in the water does not get near the propeller. Ideally, the engine should be stopped when the boat is alongside the person, prior to lifting them aboard. It is very easy for a swimmer's legs to be swept under the boat in any sort of a seaway and, if the propeller is running, that could be disastrous.

A couple of strong hands will be required to lift the person onto the deck, particularly if he or she is injured or unconscious.

Picking up a man overboard when under sail can be difficult (see panel), which is why many experienced sailors maintain that the first step when anyone falls overboard is to start the motor.

Immediately the 'man overboard!' cry goes up, the dan buoy should be deployed and one of the crew designated to act as a lookout while the boat prepares for the recovery.

The man overboard button records the yacht's position in the event of an incident.

PROCEDURE FOR PICKING UP A MAN OVERBOARD WHEN UNDER SAIL

1. Immediately the alarm is sounded, throw a life ring and dan buoy overboard. Post one of the crew to keep sight of the person in the water, as it is easy to lose sight of a someone among the waves.

2. If the boat is sailing to windward, ease the sheets and turn the bow off the wind, turning through the reaching and running stages until the boat has gybed and is downwind of the person in the water.

3. If the boat is running downwind when the person goes overboard, the sheets must be brought on hard so the boat can be close-hauled back to the pick-up position. Follow the manoeuvre for sailing onto a mooring (see p53), aiming for a position downwind of the person in the water, and then rounding up with sheets free so the momentum of the boat carries it up into the wind until it slows or stops beside the man overboard. (If the boat has a spinnaker up, it must be dropped before the boat can be brought onto the wind and sailed back to the person in the water.)

4. If the boat stops short of the person in the water, a line can be thrown and he or she can be hauled to the side before being lifted up on deck. As there is no propeller to worry about, recovery can take place anywhere along the side of the hull.

RECOVERY

Recovering a person from the water can sometimes be difficult, especially if the topsides of the boat are high and/or he or she is overweight. Even in the best conditions, pulling a waterlogged body aboard needs strong arms. When the boat is wallowing in a seaway, there is always the risk of injury due to the boat colliding with the person in the water. With a heavy body, one solution is for a couple of the crew to hold him firmly by the shoulders as he faces the boat, while he swings a leg up until it can be grabbed by another of the crew. With all available hands lifting both his shoulders and leg, he can be rolled over the gunwale; an easier procedure than trying to lift him bodily out of the water.

Another system is to tie a bowline in the end of a rope and lower it into the water. The man overboard can then get his foot into the bowline and gain leverage to push himself upwards, at the same time using his arms to pull himself up on the main part of the rope, rather like using a rope ladder or scrambling net. With head and shoulders out of the water, the weight comes off his body and the rescue becomes much easier for those on board.

If the person in the water is unconscious, the recovery process becomes very difficult. One or two of the crew should don life jackets and clip on harnesses, then jump

Recovering someone from the water requires considerable strength. Using a winch is preferable to relying on manpower alone, particularly if the yacht has a high freeboard.

into the water to support his body and secure a rope around it. A bowline passed over his shoulders and under his arms may enable him to pulled physically up the side of the boat, otherwise a halyard must be shackled on to the rope and a winch used to lift him from the water. Care must be taken that the bowline is a snug fit and does not slip; another bowline under his thighs or a bowline on a bight may hold his body more securely while being lifted aboard.

One alternative, if it can be rigged, is to use a small headsail or spinnaker as a sling, wrapping it around the unconscious body and using a halyard secured to two corners to lift him out. Another is to inflate the life raft and effect the rescue from that. Because varying conditions may be experienced when pulling a person from the water in a seaway, a little ingenuity may be required in order to adapt these basic systems to suit each individual situation.

Capsizing

It is virtually impossible for a yacht with a ballast keel to capsize and stay capsized. In an exceptionally large seaway a yacht can be rolled right over, even pitch-poled, but it cannot remain upside down as long as the keel is still attached, and a keel breaking off is unlikely. As the boat goes over, the weight of the ballast in the keel, plus the loss of wind pressure in the sails brings it back upright. Of course, if it has made a 360 degree roll, there is every possibility that the mast will have broken off and the sails and rigging will be in the water. But short of suffering some damage which allows water to access the inside of the boat, the hull should remain intact and provide a sound survival platform for the crew.

However, centreboard dinghies, catamarans and other small craft can and do capsize. Lacking a ballast keel or some other form of righting moment, they are vulnerable as soon as the centre of gravity is displaced too far (see p11). Unless the crew swings out over the side, or the sheets are eased to spill wind, the boat will capsize and either fill with water or turn turtle and stay upside down. Fortunately, most small boats can be righted, bailed out and sailed off.

Catamarans are more difficult to right because of their broad beam, but experienced crews can usually get them up and sailing again if the conditions are moderate.

Capsizing when racing a catamaran is almost part of the fun, but it is important to know how to right it before taking to deep waters, particularly if the weather is less than perfect.

A capsize can be caused by any number of factors, such as pushing the boat too hard through strong, gusty winds, a bad gybe or simply being caught unawares by a squall.

To experienced dinghy sailors, a capsize is part of the fun of sailing although it can be unnerving to the uninitiated, especially if it occurs in strong weather, or they find themselves underneath the boat and tangled in rigging. But, provided the boat is fitted with buoyancy, it should remain afloat, allowing the crew to hang on to the hull while sorting out the gear and preparing to right the boat.

The procedure for righting a capsized dinghy will depend on the type of hull. Sit-in dinghies, such as the International Mirror, will fill with water when capsized and must be righted and held in position while the water is bailed out, whereas sit-on boats, such as the Laser, have enclosed hulls so the water drains off as soon as they are righted and they are ready to sail off again.

One of the hazards of the boat turning completely upside down is the possibility, in shallow water, of the mast touching the bottom and snapping off. Under these circumstances, it is important to get the boat onto its side as soon as possible before continuing the righting procedure. In some craft, a total capsize can cause the centreboard to slip backwards out of its casing, leaving the skipper with no righting lever to get the boat back upright. Someone has to swim under the boat and replace the centreboard in its casing so the righting procedure can be started.

To right a sit-on dinghy, use your body-weight to begin the righting procedure.

THE USUAL ROUTINE FOR RIGHTING A CAPSIZED SIT-IN BOAT IS AS FOLLOWS:

1. If the boat is completely upside down, one of the crew must scramble onto the hull and grab the centreboard. By leaning backwards, the crew's weight should gradually bring the boat to the horizontal position, where rigging and sails can be sorted out. It is important that the sails are dropped, or the sheets freed, before the boat comes upright or the sails will fill with wind and the boat will either take off or capsize again. The forward hand swims round to the bow and hangs onto it, holding the boat head to wind.

Keep the bow to the wind as you start to manoeuvre the boat over.

2. The skipper climbs onto the centreboard and grasps the gunwale, leaning back again and pulling the boat into the upright position. With the forward hand holding the bow into the wind and the sails free to flap, the boat should just sit quietly in the water, although it will be full of water.

Stand on the centreboard to help gain momentum as the sails come free.

3. The skipper scrambles aboard over the stern and begins to bail out some of the water, while the forward hand remains in the water still holding the bow into the wind. As soon as the water level inside the boat has dropped, the skipper sorts out any tangled ropes, pulls on the mainsail and brings the helm to windward so the boat's head bears away from the wind.

4. The forward hand now scrambles aboard over the windward side and sheets on the jib, at the same time continuing with the bailing process. If a vortex bailer is fitted, it can be opened as soon as the boat picks up speed and the remainder of the water sucked out. It is important to remember that when full, or nearly full, of water, the boat will be very unstable and great care will be necessary to prevent it capsizing again, either as a result of wind and wave, or the actions of the crew scrambling aboard.

Quickly scramble aboard as the boat begins to right itself.

When the worst happens and you lose your mast, it can take some ingenuity and practical resourcefulness to ensure that you are able to return safely to port under jury rig.

Dismasting

When the rigging gives way and the mast falls over the side, the boat loses its main source of power. With most large yachts, this means starting up the motor, but with centreboarders and other small craft, it means getting out the paddles. In sheltered waters dismasting is usually not too dramatic an event, although it can entail an embarrassing, and often very public, return to the clubhouse minus everything above deck! However, dismasting on the open ocean is a different matter. If it happens when the boat is beyond the range of rescue services, and for some reason the motor cannot be used, there is no alternative but to sail home under jury rig.

In all cases, the most important move is to get the fallen mast and rigging aboard or, if that is not possible, cut it loose. The boat will make no headway under motor or paddles with a mess of mast and rigging dragging through the water. In the case of small craft, the debris can usually be lifted aboard, as it is fairly light and manageable, but with larger yachts it may be necessary to cut it loose, to prevent it fouling the propeller. Save any spars of a reasonable length, including the broken mast, as they may come in useful for the jury rig.

It goes without saying that a sea-going yacht's toolbox must contain wire cutters, hacksaw and an axe.

JURY RIG

If a substantial section of the mast is still standing, a compromise rig can usually be made with the normal sails, albeit reduced in size, which will enable to boat to make moderate progress downwind and perhaps even to a degree across wind. But if the mast is little more than a stump, a jury rig will need to be made up of the spars that are left on board. As a general rule, this rig will only enable the boat to progress on a broad reach or run.

A jury rig is simply the best possible rig that can be made out of whatever can be recovered from the original rig. The remains of the original mast, spinnaker poles or booms can be utilized if they are undamaged. The longest should be lashed to the mast stump and supported by shrouds and stays cut from the original standing rigging. Sails, too, may need to be folded or cut to fit the jury rig.

Innovation is the key factor in re-rigging a dismasted boat, using anything that is available to get the boat moving again.

When a boat is deeper aft than forward, moving weight to the bow can sometimes help to free the keel.

One way to increase the heel of a boat that is stranded on mud or sand, is to use the tender to run an anchor some distance from the boat. Attaching a halyard to the anchor and tensioning it with a winch will pull the top of the mast down and create more heel.

Hanging a weight (or a member of the crew) from the boom end may heel the boat enough to float it free.

Grounding and stranding

Almost as inevitable as running out of gas in the car, is running aground in a boat. With sailing dinghies, trailer-sailers and cata-marans which are designed to be beached, there is normally no problem, but with fixed keel yachts the problems can be very signifi-cant. First and foremost, there is the damage that may be inflicted on the keel or the structure of the hull by the impact of grounding, and secondly, there is the question

of refloating, which can lead to damage to the hull skin or stress on the hull if the boat is towed off. The worst-case scenario is being stranded on a falling tide because, if the tide drops far enough, the yacht will fall over on its side and fill with water before it can be refloated on the next tide.

A simple grounding, on a soft sandy or muddy bottom, should not create too much difficulty. The sails must be lowered immediately to prevent the boat driving further aground, and the motor started

and engaged in reverse. If this does not work, the crew must move to one side – even hanging out on the boom – to heel the boat over as far as possible. This uses the buoyancy of the bilge to help lift the keel off the bottom.

If the boat still remains stuck fast, the heel must be increased. One way to achieve this is by running a halyard ashore to a convenient tree or rock, or running an anchor out some distance from the boat and securing a halyard to it. When the halyard is tensioned with a winch it

If going aground is unavoidable, every attempt should be made to prop the boat upright as the tide falls, otherwise it is likely to fill with water when the tide rises again.

A boat leaning towards the sea will flood when the next tide comes in.

This boat has been heeled so the cabin faces away from the incoming tide.

will pull the top of the mast down and heel the boat over even more. If this fails, however, the situation is serious and some outside help will probably be needed to tow the boat off. Unfortunately, help is not always available, or at best could take time to arrive.

In the meantime the tide will be dropping, leaving the boat in danger of falling on its side, where nothing short of a sizeable crane will lift it up again.

The immediate need is to hold the boat upright as the tide falls. This can be achieved by propping up the hull with whatever spars or props are available, such as the spinnaker pole. By driving these into the sea bed and securing them under the gunwales on either side, there is a chance of holding the boat upright as the water level drops – provided the makeshift supports won't collapse under the boat's weight.

Keel yachts that sail frequently in high-range tidal waters often carry a couple of props for this purpose. While propping up the boat won't solve the problem of getting it afloat again, it at least prevents it from falling onto its side and filling with water on the next incoming tide which, hopefully, will be high enough to lift the boat off. (Don't forget to close the seacocks and drains, to prevent incoming water from flooding the hull.)

Novice sailors are likely to experience some moments of panic when they encounter their first serious incident at sea, but all sailors soon learn to distinguish between stormy, if uncomfortable, conditions and those that might at any moment become life-threatening.

Abandon ship!

These are the words every sailor dreads hearing. When all else fails, and every attempt has been made to save the boat, the time has come to abandon it and embrace some form of rescue. It is important to remember, however, that this is an absolute last resort. Over the years, a number of yachtsmen and women have been lost by abandoning their boats too soon, only for the boats to be found days later, still afloat and, in some cases, virtually intact; had the crew stayed aboard they would probably have survived. This was brought home very forcibly in the 1979 Fastnet

Race disaster when 15 lives were lost, yet 18 yachts were later found abandoned but afloat. One can only wonder how many of those sailors would have survived had they remained with their boats.

In any emergency, one of the most dangerous factors is panic. Inexperienced sailors caught in a big storm will understandably panic when they see water inside the boat, yet it is surprising how much water can enter a hull before the boat is likely to sink. Fear of the unknown, exacerbated by dramatic wind and sea conditions, plays havoc with novice nerves and it is important for the skipper and

experienced crew members to take charge and calm any panic before it gets out of hand.

Keeping nervous crew occupied is one way of overcoming panic. If there is water in the boat, set up a chain gang in the cabin; filling buckets and passing them up the companionway will keep minds and bodies busy. Whether this succeeds in bailing out the boat or not will depend on circumstances, but certainly it will help distract nervous crew members from worrying about what might occur.

If the worst happens and there is no hope of saving the boat, then an orderly procedure for abandoning

A training exercise, conducted by the local sea rescue service, helps to familiarize yacht crews with the workings of the life raft, teaching them how to inflate it and board it, as well as what to do in the event that they ever have to abandon ship.

it must be followed to ensure that everyone survives.

A radio call for assistance should already have been sent to rescue organizations (see p100). This must be upgraded to advise them of the boat's position and the latest developments, which by now will have reached Mayday status.

When help arrives, it will be in the form of rescue boats or helicopters. The operation will likely be directed by the rescuers and the crew must follow instructions quickly and positively. Never challenge an order, otherwise confusion will result and, in emergency circumstances, confusion can mean disaster.

If there is no outside help, then the skipper must take control and instruct the crew on the procedure for abandoning the yacht. The life raft is inflated and launched, taking care to tie it securely to the yacht otherwise it may blow away and be lost before anyone gets into it. The grab bag is stowed in the raft together with flares and any emergency items that are not already on board. Fresh water is essential for survival, and containers should be stowed in the raft, together with the EPIRB, which should have been activated to guide rescue craft. Finally, the crew must clamber into the life raft, secure its canopy, and

untie the life raft from the yacht as soon as it is obvious that the yacht is about to sink.

HELICOPTER RESCUE

A rescue by surface craft will almost certainly be directed by the rescuers, but in the case of a helicopter rescue, the crew of the yacht should know in advance what they will be required to do.

The mast and rigging, if it is still standing, will be swaying wildly as the boat wallows in the seaway, and can endanger the helicopter if its winch wire becomes entangled in the rigging. There is also considerable risk for the winch man as he

Coastguard and rescue services regularly carry out drills to train their helicopter crews for emergency rescues, which seldom take place under such calm conditions as these!

is lowered, so the rescue procedure usually takes place well away from the boat. The yacht's crew will need to either jump overboard on the end of a line and drift astern of the stricken yacht, where they can be safely plucked from the sea, or climb into the life raft which will also be allowed to drift astern of the yacht so the rescue can be carried out in clear air.

A rescue at sea is always traumatic but, by knowing what they are required to do in the event of a helicopter rescue, sailors can make the often-difficult task of the emergency fliers much easier and safer which, in turn, improves their own chances of survival.

Fire on board

There is nothing more frightening than a fire on board, particularly when you are a long way from shore. A boat has a lot of flammable material in its hull and fittings, to say nothing of fuel tanks and LPG bottles, making it a virtual floating bomb if fire breaks out.

With the correct precautions, the risks can be reduced, if not eliminated, but the unexpected can still happen and, once a fire starts on board, it can be difficult to control. There are no speedy fire engines at sea and even if there were, by the time they reached the scene the fire would have made short work of the boat. As far as the crew are concerned, they are virtually

trapped, since they can't walk away from a burning boat as they might from a fire on shore.

As always, prevention is better than cure. The better the boat and crew are prepared, the faster any on-board fire can be controlled and extinguished. Correct fire-fighting procedures, the right gear and a sound knowledge of the characteristics and behaviour of fires are three essential factors in any fire-related emergency. The first step in prevention is to understand what causes a fire and to ensure that, if one breaks out, it is controlled as fast as possible.

Obviously fuel creates the highest risk and must be handled with great care at all times. Fuel tanks must be correctly installed and vented outside the hull. Fuel that is spilled when refuelling can make its way into the bilges where it lies like a time bomb, waiting for a spark to ignite it. Sniffer detectors in the bilges will sound the alarm immediately a build-up of gas is detected and should be fitted in every boat where fuel is carried.

LPG creates similar dangers, so all gas piping should be installed by a licensed plumber and the gas bottles carried in vented lockers on deck, not down below.

The best fire-fighting methods can be gleaned from a study of the fire triangle (see opposite). One side of the triangle is fuel, another is oxygen and the third is a source of ignition, such as a spark or

THE FIRE TRIANGLE

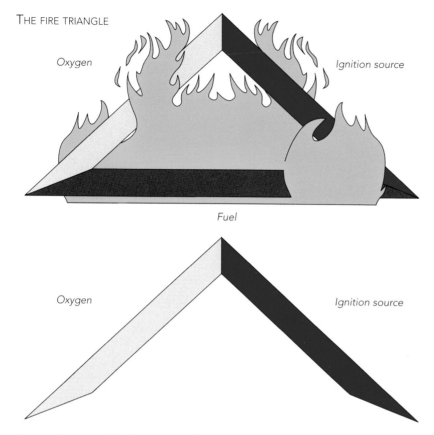

By removing one of the elements – fuel, oxygen or the ignition source – from the fire triangle you can extinguish a fire.

flame. For a fire to exist, all three must be present; if you remove any side of the triangle, the fire will be extinguished. Successful fire-fighting revolves around which is the best or easiest side to remove.

If there is no fuel there is nothing to burn, without a spark or flame (ignition) the fuel, however volatile, will not catch fire, and without air (oxygen) a fire will be smothered. Successful fire-fighting relies on the removal of one of these factors.

For example, take a yacht galley with a pan of hot oil on the stove, ready to cook the evening meal. If the oil catches fire, the fire triangle is called into play to determine which of the three sides to remove. Since the oil is already alight, it is too late to remove the ignition, which leaves two options; remove the fuel or remove the oxygen.

Throwing the pan overboard will remove the fuel, so that is one option. If that is not possible it leaves the removal of air as the only way to fight the fire, and the best way to do this is with a fire-retardant blanket.

Despite water being an excellent fire extinguisher, and despite having an abundance of it around the boat, water cannot be used on fat or oil fires as the oil will spatter and spread when it comes into contact with water. Many chemical, or dry powder, fire-extinguishers are unsuitable for use in the confined space of a yacht's interior because of the toxic gas they give off. Foam is effective for oil fires, but it should only be used where there is good ventilation.

When it comes to choosing fire-extinguishers for your boat, it is worth obtaining specialist advice with regard to the type, size and ideal placement of the canisters. One solution is to have different fire-fighting systems capable of coping with engine, galley and cabin fires.

As with most other on-board emergencies, an important factor when faced with a fire is to remain calm and avoid panic. This is not easy, because the interior of a yacht is a very confined space, and confronting a fire down below can be terrifying, so a cool head is as important as the correct extinguisher. Assess the situation, send out a distress call if need be, determine which approach to the fire will be most effective, then tackle it firmly and positively.

If the fire gets out of control and there is no hope of saving the boat, prepare the life raft in good time so that the crew will be able to abandon the boat before the fire reaches the fuel tanks.

There is always a risk of hypothermia (exposure to extreme cold) when someone has been washed overboard, but when there are other injuries present, the risk increases dramatically, so great care must be taken to keep a casualty warm while treating their injuries.

First aid at sea

Most medical emergencies afloat are the result of accidents, ranging from lacerations and broken bones through near drowning to serious internal or head injuries. Whatever the cause, appropriate first aid treatment should be carried out on the spot to prevent the condition worsening. Even if the boat is relatively close to shore, it may be some time before medical assistance can be obtained.

Modern telecommunications, the longer patrol range of rescue vessels, and the increasing use of helicopters carrying paramedics have all reduced the odds of a casualty being too long without specialized care, but even so, the quick and correct application of first aid can make even a serious accident more manageable.

While sailors who never venture beyond coastal waters are usually within reach of help, when it comes to sailing offshore or crossing oceans, it is a wise skipper who ensures that he and one or more of his crew are trained in first aid, and able to administer CPR and other life-saving procedures.

Emergency communication systems

A vital part of an emergency at sea is the availability of good communication systems so that help can be obtained if things get serious. Provided the right system is used, there should be no reason for any vessel requiring assistance failing to make contact with an official rescue organization.

Modern satellite systems have brought increased reliability and sophistication to maritime communications. Where the previous radio systems suffered from mostly terrestrial (earth-bound) problems that caused interference with signals, satellites, being outside earth's influence, provide superior signals almost anywhere on earth.

The Comsat (satellite communications) system beams a signal on UHF directly to a satellite that is above the horizon, which sends it back down to a receiving station on land from where it can be fed into the normal telephone system or a satellite phone network.

This system is so simple and efficient that the widely used GSM cellphone network can sometimes be used at sea for normal voice, fax or data services, as well as text messages and emails.

GMDSS

The Global Maritime Distress and Safety System (GMDSS), the current medium for handling distress calls at sea, has replaced older systems whereby shore stations kept a listening watch over high frequency (HF), medium frequency (MF) and very high frequency (VHF) radio channels for distress calls. GMDSS was introduced in 1999 and provides automatic monitoring of distress calls using special Digital Selective Calling (DSC) channels. When a distress signal is received on any frequency, it automatically indicates the boat's call sign. Using satellite and land-based services, it enables a fix of the boat's position to be determined, at the same time alerting rescue organizations.

Conventional distress listening watches on the various radio frequencies will be phased out during 2005, after which the International Maritime Organization (IMO) plans for GMDSS to take over all distress monitoring. Because the switch to the new system is fairly expensive, many boat owners will continue using the old systems until GMDSS is fully operational, and it may take some time before it becomes universal.

GMDSS is divided into zones which extend outward from the coast, as indicated in the illustration below.

Sea zones covered by GMDSS

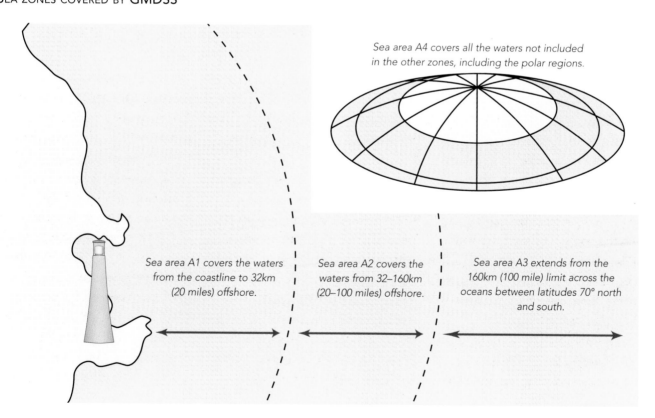

Sea area A4 covers all the waters not included in the other zones, including the polar regions.

Sea area A1 covers the waters from the coastline to 32km (20 miles) offshore.

Sea area A2 covers the waters from 32–160km (20–100 miles) offshore.

Sea area A3 extends from the 160km (100 mile) limit across the oceans between latitudes 70° north and south.

Inmarsat Mini-M

Inmarsat stands for International Maritime Satellite Corporation, a major consortium that operates an extensive satellite communications network across the world. As with other Comsat systems, transmissions from a boat are beamed to one of the active satellites and then bounced back to a receiving station on land.

There are a number of Inmarsat receivers designed for specific uses. Inmarsat M is most widely used for marine communications and is popular with boat owners as it is relatively small and compact.

Inmarsat C is used for sending and receiving email and text messages from vessels at sea.

When making an emergency radio call, it is important to give the boat's position as accurately as possible.

Emergency radio calls

There are many ways in which a vessel in distress can call for help. Most common are emergency radio calls, although some visual signals are important when rescue is within reach (see opposite).

Radio distress calls can be transmitted on any frequency, but they have the best chance of being heard if they are put out over the main calling channels (VHF channels 16 and 2182, or DSC channel 70).

A permanent listening watch is kept on many ships and most shore stations on all radio frequencies. Immediately a Mayday call is heard, all other radio traffic ceases until the emergency is over. To ensure that distress calls are not drowned out by normal radio chatter, a three minute silence is maintained on the major channels, usually on the hour and half hour. Distress calls include:

Mayday – The internationally recognized distress signal for grave or imminent danger to a vessel or its crew. Repeat three times, followed by the vessel's position repeated three times and details related to the emergency. Mayday is only to be used in cases of extreme distress, where there is an immediate threat to life.

Pan – The international urgency call. Also repeated three times. Pan is used when a vessel is in danger and there is a potential for loss of life, but the situation is not sufficiently serious to warrant a Mayday call.

Securitay/securité – Used as a safety signal, or to warn shipping of hazards, often navigational, which could create a danger to vessels, but which pose no immediate threat to life.

When making an emergency call, it is important to provide accurate information so that rescuers do not waste time trying to locate you. You need to convey the boat's position as accurately as possible (ideally taken off your GPS or last known log entry), provide the boat's name and registration details if asked for them, and give information about the nature of the assistance required and the number of people on board. Even when the situation is dire, try to speak slowly and clearly, particularly if you do not speak the same language as the rescue services you are approaching for help.

Visual signals

These are obviously only of use when the shore or other craft are close at hand. While various systems are used around the world and on different classes of vessels, the following standard signals for small craft in most countries are certain to attract attention:

Rocket flares: Hand-held mini smoke flares or rocket flares will attract attention from quite some distance away. Usually red, they are the most commonly used visual distress signal. Before setting off a flare, remember that any rescuers will be scanning a large area of sky and may be looking in the other direction as your signal goes up, so it is best to send up two or three flares in quick succession.

Take note of the wind direction before releasing a rocket flare, making sure you are on the downwind side of the boat, and that the flare will not hit any sails or rigging as it is fired. Keep hand-held flares away from your face and body.

Unless you have a large supply of flares, delay using them until you are fairly sure that they will be seen by rescuers in the area. Use smoke signals during the day and flares at night.

Remember that rocket flares can become very hot, so be careful not to burn yourself or accidentally drop a flare, as it could start a fire – not a desirable situation when you are at sea.

SOS: Flashed with a torch, this traditional distress signal is limited by the range of the torch light. The SOS signal (... _ _ _ ...) comprises three short flashes of light, followed by three longer flashes, and a further three short flashes, repeated at intervals. The same pattern can also be made with sounds, using an air horn or whistle.

Heliograph mirror: This special instrument with mirrors and a shutter is used for sending messages in morse code, but any shiny surface can be utilized to reflect sunlight, creating a surprisingly powerful flash in the eyes of rescuers. Mirrors are particularly effective for signalling to searching aircraft, and life rafts always carry a polished plate and signalling stick.

Orange 'V' sheet: This is a large sheet of plastic or lightweight fabric that is spread out on deck or over the coach roof. The colour contrasts vividly with the blue and white of the ocean when seen from the air, enabling aircraft to spot a disabled vessel more quickly. ('V' is the code flag indicating that assistance is required, see p81.)

Bucket of burning oily rags: While not a widely accepted distress signal, the black smoke given off by burning oil can be seen from afar and is effective in attracting attention. Needless to say the bucket must be made of steel, not plastic!

Signal flags: The International Code Flags NC (N above C) are a universal distress sign (see p81).

Training exercises enable sailors to become familiar with emergency procedures, such as setting off flares, and experiencing conditions in a life raft at sea in the dark.

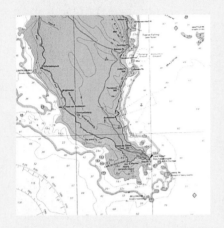  

PILOTAGE

Pilotage can be described as the art of visual navigation. Although instruments can be, and often are, used, for the most part pilotage involves negotiating harbours, estuaries and close inshore waters by using buoys, beacons, lights and other visual means. Coastal navigation usually begins at a departure position outside the harbour or estuary and involves laying and steering courses along the coastline (see p121) but, prior to that, the boat may have to be taken downstream, or out through the harbour entrance, and this is where pilotage is involved. Hazards in sheltered waters must be negotiated by following buoys and other marks that indicate channels and provide the navigator with a safe passage into open waters.

In many parts of the world, yachts have to clear tidal estuaries, river mouths or harbours before coastal navigation begins.

Tides and tidal streams

Pilotage has to take account of tides and tidal streams, the effects of which are most pronounced in inshore waters, particularly rivers and estuaries. Being shallow, these areas create hazards that can be exacerbated by tidal influences, and the navigator must be aware of features such as the bar across a river mouth, which can be dangerous and, in most cases, should be crossed only on a flood tide.

Working with tide tables, a chart of the waterway, and with the buoys and beacons that provide visual assistance, pilotage into and out of a harbour or estuary should not create any great problems for an experienced navigator.

About 75 per cent of the world's surface is covered by sea, so it follows that tides and tidal streams affect most inshore waters.

Tides are created by the gravitational effect of the moon (and, to a lesser extent, the sun) pulling up the water into a tidal wave which travels around the globe every 24 hours, as the world turns. This is not the tidal wave of movies, which is in fact a tsunami. Instead, it is a more modest wave, around two metres (6ft) high, and spread over a vast ocean area.

At sea the wave would not be noticeable, but when it reaches the coast it normally manifests itself as a slow rise and fall of water levels, reaching its peak at high tide and

its lowest point at low tide. Because a second tidal wave forms on the opposite side of the globe, most coastal regions experience two high and two low tides every day.

On some coastlines, the land mass creates obstructions which can cause the tidal wave to change character quite considerably. For example, the Isle of Wight, off the south coast of England, divides each incoming tidal wave into two separate waves, which reach the inshore port of Southampton at different times, thus creating four high tides each day, instead of the usual two.

The tidal wave rolling into the Bay of Fundy, off Nova Scotia and New Brunswick on Canada's east

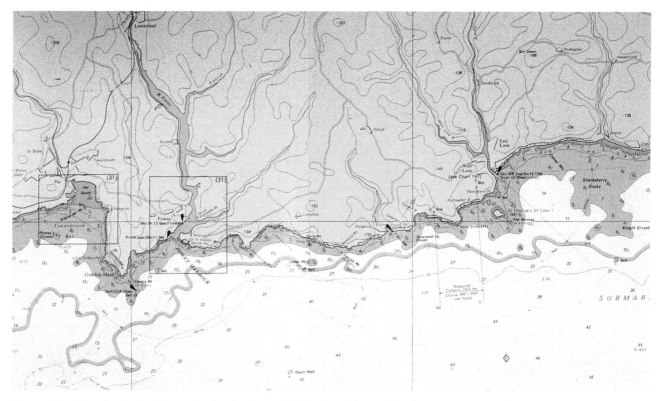

On a marine chart, the depth of the sea bed at the lowest tide is indicated by a series of continuous contour lines.

coast, passes through a bottleneck which compresses it, resulting in extremely high and low tides.

A similar topographical phenomenon occurs off Australia's northern coast. Here, it causes the coastal waters to dry out at low tide for many kilometres offshore. When the tide turns, the incoming water races in at such a speed that where it runs between two islands it has two different levels, creating what is known as the 'horizontal waterfall'! Although these are extremes, even normal tidal flows can present navigational dangers for vessels sailing inshore. Tidal flow charts and tide tables are used to determine anything that might affect navigation in an estuary or harbour.

The gravitational pull of the sun and moon varies according to their position relative to the earth. When the sun and moon are on the same side of the earth (pulling in conjunction) or on diametrically opposite sides (pulling in opposition), their combined gravitational pull is strongest and causes the water to pile up higher than usual.

When the sun and moon pull at right angles to one another, the effect is reduced and the tidal range is lower. (See also p55.)

Thus, twice a month, at new moon and full moon, the tidal wave is at its highest (this is known as spring tide). In the first and third quarter phases, the lesser tides are called neap tides.

CHART DATUM

To provide a base level for tidal calculations, the lowest mean level of the neap tide is adopted, and it is the standard on which the depths marked on charts are determined. It is known as chart datum and is an important safety factor, for it means that at almost all times, there will be more water over the sea bed than is marked on the chart.

Therefore, to find the exact depth of water over the bottom at any given time, the tide height for that period (taken from the tide tables for the area) must be added to the depth marked on the chart.

TIDE TABLES

Tidal predictions appear in books of tide tables for most of the major waterways in the world. Official tide tables, usually produced by the hydrographic office, list times and heights of high and low water for major ports, with a supplementary list covering lesser ports. Privately produced commercial tide tables are often more relevant for local conditions, although they are generally adapted from the official tide tables.

Buoys and beacons

Harbours and estuaries can be a navigator's nightmare, with hazards such as shoals and reefs, tide runs and narrow channels, plus the presence of waterborne traffic such as ferries and commercial shipping. To assist with navigation, most waterways are marked with a system of buoys or beacons (for daytime use) and special lights (that are used at night). A sound knowledge of these systems is essential if pilotage problems are to be avoided.

The International Association of Lighthouse Authorities (IALA) controls the buoyage systems used globally. There are two main systems, or zones: the IALA Zone B covers North and South America, Japan, Korea and the Philippines, while IALA Zone A covers Europe and the rest of the world.

There are other local areas which may use individual systems of their own but, for the most part, the

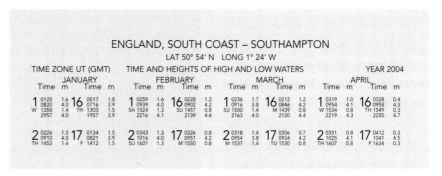

ENGLAND, SOUTH COAST – SOUTHAMPTON
LAT 50° 54' N   LONG 1° 24' W
TIME ZONE UT (GMT)   TIME AND HEIGHTS OF HIGH AND LOW WATERS   YEAR 2004

	JANUARY Time m		JANUARY Time m		FEBRUARY Time m		FEBRUARY Time m		MARCH Time m		MARCH Time m		APRIL Time m		APRIL Time m
1 W	0125 1.6 / 0820 4.0 / 1358 1.4 / 2957 4.0	**16** TH	0017 1.8 / 0716 3.9 / 1303 1.5 / 1957 3.9	**1** SA	0259 1.6 / 0939 4.0 / 1524 1.3 / 2216 4.1	**16** SU	0228 1.2 / 0902 4.2 / 1457 0.8 / 2139 4.4	**1** M	0236 1.7 / 0916 3.8 / 1500 1.4 / 2163 4.0	**16** TU	0212 1.2 / 0846 4.2 / 1439 0.8 / 2120 4.4	**1** W	0319 1.0 / 0954 4.1 / 1534 0.8 / 2219 4.3	**16** TH	0328 0.4 / 0958 4.5 / 1549 0.3 / 2220 4.7
2 TH	0226 1.5 / 0910 4.0 / 1453 1.4	**17** F	0134 1.5 / 0821 3.9 / 1412 1.5	**2** SU	0343 1.3 / 1016 4.0 / 1601 1.3	**17** M	0326 0.8 / 0951 4.2 / 1550 0.8	**2** TU	0318 1.4 / 0954 3.8 / 1537 1.4	**17** W	0306 0.7 / 0934 4.2 / 1530 0.8	**2** TH	0351 0.8 / 1025 4.1 / 1607 0.8	**17** F	0412 0.3 / 1041 4.5 / 1634 0.3

On a coastal passage, the navigator will need to refer constantly to the tide tables.

IALA systems are accepted as standard for the maritime world. Both involve the use of two major buoyage systems: the Lateral system and the Cardinal system.

LATERAL SYSTEM

When a boat enters a strange harbour or estuary it is important to know where the channels lie, as well as the location of any navigational hazards such as sandbanks, reefs or wrecks. The lateral system uses coloured buoys and beacons to guide boats through channels and past dangers to clear water, where navigation is safe.

Unfortunately, these buoys are not standardized throughout all waterways. In fact, the systems used in IALA Zone B are often the opposite of those used in Zone A.

With both systems, however, all marks are read when entering a port from seaward. In Zone A, red buoys, beacons and lights indicate the left or port side of the channel and must be left to the port side, while green marks indicate the right or starboard side of the channel or danger and must be left to starboard side.

Top and centre: Buoys may be numbered for easy reference on local charts.
Bottom: Larger buoys may be used to mark offshore shoals, or indicate 'landfall'.

Lights and lighthouses

Lights and lighthouses are the sailor's signposts. By day, a lighthouse structure is readily identifiable, providing an accurate point of reference for navigation. By night, the light serves the same purpose, guiding the mariner along the coastline, into harbours and estuaries, and through the maze of inshore channels to a safe anchorage or berth. For this reason, all navigation lights are very clearly and positively marked on the chart, together with a wealth of information about them. There are three principal types of lights used for navigation:

The Fastnet Light, a powerful ocean light situated some 18.5km (10 nautical miles) off the southern coast of Ireland, is a familiar sight to sailors participating in the eponymous race.

The powerful beam of an ocean light must be visible for many kilometres offshore.

OCEAN LIGHTS

Long-range lights are located strategically along most coastlines, to provide reference points for the navigator making his way along the coast, or for vessels making a landfall after an ocean passage. Ocean lights may also warn of dangerous shoals or reefs in inshore waters.

Often situated on headlands or capes, they may have a range of 25 nautical miles or more and mostly employ a rotating beam with a powerful fresnel lens positioned at the top of a high tower or structure, which is usually painted white to make it stand out against the cliffs or vegetation of the coastline.

As the beam sweeps across the sea, it passes over the boat, from where it is seen as a bright flash, like someone flashing a torch in your eyes.

COASTAL LIGHTS

These are usually medium-power lights with a range of around 5–10 nautical miles, which guide vessels into a harbour or estuary. They are mostly located near the entrance to the harbour and shine to seaward, providing guidance for boats approaching the harbour either from along the coast or from the open sea.

Coastal lights use many different guidance systems to provide the navigator with accurate alignment past the hazards or dangers in the harbour approach channels. Two of the systems commonly used are leading lights (also known as range lights), and sectored lights, which may be coloured to indicate specific dangers (see p111).

HARBOUR LIGHTS

These indicate both the navigation channels and any dangers found within harbours and estuaries. They may be located either on the shore or on buoys and beacons, and use various colours, mostly white, red and green.

Harbour lights usually have a fairly short range (1–10 nautical miles) and are identified by the flashing characteristics of an individual light. Once inside a harbour

The narrow entrance to a small harbour is indicated by port and starboard lights. These are always positioned as they would be seen from the sea, or incoming, side.

entrance, the navigator depends on the lights to guide him past inshore hazards, such as shoals, shallow water or restricted areas, and along channels that will lead to his berth or an anchorage.

In major ports, lights may be used to indicate the movements of incoming or outbound ships, with different colours and flashing sequences indicating where the activity is taking place.

Harbour lights are sometimes located on floating buoys.

Light characteristics

Every navigation light has a unique characteristic by which it can be identified. Apart from using different colours, each light flashes in a distinctive way, some with short flashes, some with long, some with one flash, some with groups of flashes. The flashes are repeated in cycles. When navigating, the 'identity' of a particular light can be determined by both the type of flashing and the timing of the flash cycle.

Below are some of the principal characteristics used, and the abbreviations by which these are indicated on charts:

F – Fixed Showing a constant, unbroken light.

Fl – Flashing The period of light is shorter than the period of darkness.

Q – Quick Rapid flashing, at a rate of about 50–80 per minute.

Oc – Occulting The period of light is longer than the period of darkness.

Fl (2) – Group flashing The light is seen in groups of flashes, usually 2, 3 or 4, as indicated.

Alt – Alternating Flashing or occulting in alternating colours.

Oc (2) – Group occulting The light is seen in groups of occults, as indicated.

Iso – Isophase Length of the flash is the same as the length of darkness.

The timing of the flashing cycle is indicated on the chart in an abbreviated form, as is the colour of the light, its range (distance it is visible) and its height above sea level.

For example, a white light situated 90m (295ft) above sea level, flashing in groups of four every 15 seconds with a range of five nautical miles would appear on the chart as *Fl (4)15s 90m 5M*.

(If there is no indication of colour, the light is white. Red and green lights carry the letters R and G respectively.)

Leading lights and transit beacons make it easier to steer a course through a harbour channel. At night, lead lights are aligned in the same way as beacons are during the day.

Guidance lights

In places where winding channels or isolated hazards make navigation particularly difficult, two light systems are used to guide vessels safely through the dangers.

LEADING (RANGE) LIGHTS

The most accurate of the two systems is known as leading or range lights. Since the lights are usually mounted on distinctive structures or shapes, they can be used by day

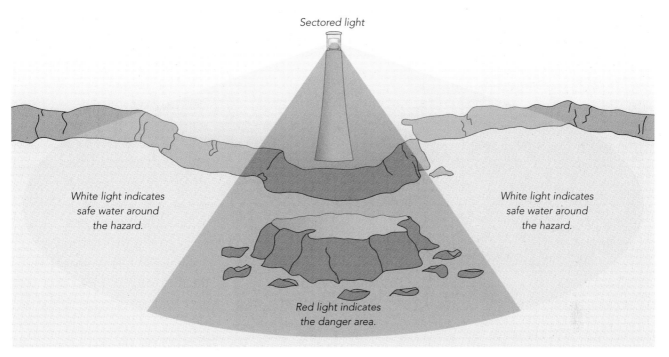

Sectored light

White light indicates safe water around the hazard.

White light indicates safe water around the hazard.

Red light indicates the danger area.

Sectored lights can be used to demarcate a coastal hazard. Coloured lights indicate the boat's position in relation to danger. Provided action is taken as soon as the adverse light (here red) appears, the boat will be able to navigate safely past the danger.

or night. Two lights are located one above the other, with the lower light in front of and some distance ahead of the upper light.

As seen from the boat, when these two lights are aligned one above the other, the boat is in the centre of the channel. If the lower light moves to the right of the upper light the boat is drifting to the left of the channel; if the lower light moves to the left of the upper light, the boat is drifting towards the right of the channel.

By day, distinctive marks replace the lights. They are usually triangular in shape, with the upper triangle mounted apex-down and the lower one apex-up. Any movement out of the channel is quickly noted as the apexes move apart. The marks

are often painted in bright, fluorescent colours to provide an accurate system of negotiating even the most tortuous channels.

This simple system is widely used on the bends of winding rivers and channels, providing a safe and easy method of navigating difficult waterways.

SECTORED LIGHTS

These lights, which are also used in coastal waters, indicate offshore hazards and dangers by covering them with a distinctive coloured light, or lights.

The lighthouse in which the lights are mounted has a normal white light but this is screened to show different colours over different areas. An offshore reef, for

example, may be covered by a red light, so that an approaching boat will see a white light as long as it is in safe water. When the light turns red, the boat has moved too close to the danger and must take avoiding action until the light turns white again.

Sectored lights are often used to provide guidance into a harbour. The boat sails across the entrance until a white light is seen, at which point it turns and heads straight for the light, which indicates the centre of the channel. If the light turns red, the boat is moving out of the channel on the port side. If it turns green the boat is to the right of the channel. By staying in the white sector the boat will enter the harbour safely in mid-stream.

COASTAL NAVIGATION

Coastal navigation can be broadly described as 'offshore navigation within sight of land'. Naturally, there may be times, such as on a long stretch of coastline or across the estuary of a big river, when land will only be a distant smudge on the horizon but, generally speaking, the traditional system of coastal navigation uses land objects as the basis of getting from one place to another. GPS provides an electronic and very accurate form of navigation which uses neither land nor celestial objects (other than man-made satellites) but, like all electronic equipment, there is always the potential for error or failure, so the traditional methods, even if not used all the time, should always be available as back-up.

Plotting a course involves using the appropriate charts, together with the relevant Sailing Directions, Pilots or other publications. Regardless of whether you are crossing oceans or sailing in familiar home waters, it is always reassuring to know where you are at sea.

Charts and chart instruments

The marine chart is the sailor's equivalent of a road map. It represents a part of the earth's surface depicted on a sheet of paper or the flat screen of a computer. Because the earth is round, this flat representation is subject to a slight distortion, which is reduced to a minimum by a system known as Mercator projection. Coastal charts cover limited areas of the earth's surface, so the distortion is small enough to be ignored, while ocean and long-distance charts are more affected by the distortion.

Charts come in a variety of scales (sizes). Small-scale charts cover large areas of the globe. They are only used for open-ocean navigation, as they provide insufficient detail for coastal navigation.

Medium-scale charts show considerable detail of coastal areas, making them ideal for navigating along stretches of coast from one port to another.

Large-scale charts give extensive detail of small areas such as harbours and estuaries, and are used by boats making into or out of sheltered waters.

Latitude and longitude

All charts have parallels of latitude and meridians of longitude drawn on them, making up a global grid. Latitude begins at 0 degrees on the equator and runs north and south to the poles, which are situated at 90 degrees latitude. A scale running down each side of the chart represents the latitude scale. The lines that run across a chart are called parallels of latitude.

Longitude begins at 0 degrees at the prime meridian (passing through Greenwich, London) and runs east and west to the 180 degree meridian on the opposite side of the globe.

The meridians of longitude are the vertical lines on the chart and the longitude scale runs across the top and bottom. Both latitude and longitude scales are in degrees and minutes of arc.

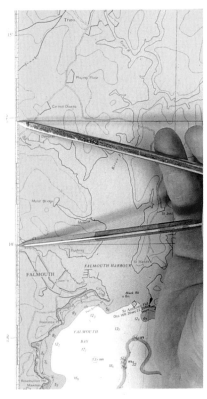

Measuring the scale with a pair of dividers.

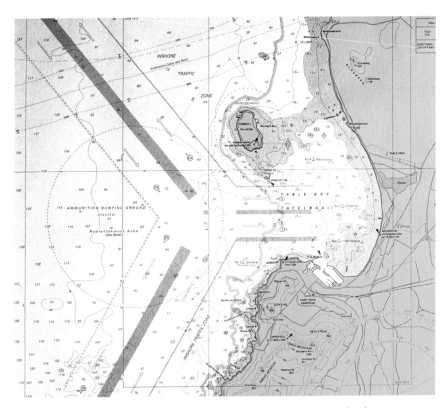

The scattered figures on the chart, known as soundings, indicate water depth in metres.

DISTANCE

While most of the world has now adopted the metric system for charts, some countries (and some older charts) still use imperial measurements, so it is important when buying a chart to check beforehand to see what measurement system is being used.

The standard measurement of distance at sea is a nautical mile (1852 metres), which equals one minute of latitude on the earth's surface. To measure distance, a pair of dividers is used to transfer the distance on the chart to the latitude scale at the side of the chart, where it can be read off in minutes of latitude and thus nautical miles.

SOUNDINGS

It is obviously important for a navigator to know exactly how much water he has under his keel, so across the entire seaward area of the chart are a mass of figures (or soundings) indicating depths in metres, decimals of a metre, or fathoms (6ft/1.8288m) and feet.

Soundings are calculated at the lowest mean tide level, known as chart datum (see p104). To find the exact depth of water at any spot, the height of the tide at the time is added to the soundings on the chart. Contour lines, similar to those used on maps to show hills and mountains, indicate the contours of the sea bed.

COMPASS ROSE

Another important feature on the chart is the compass rose, a facsimile of a standard compass card, which is used for laying off courses and bearings when navigating. A number of compass roses are located strategically across the chart so that there is always one close to where the navigator is working. Compass roses are graduated in three-figure notation from 0 degrees to 360 degrees, with 0 degrees indicating the direction of true north.

Details of the magnetic compass and the errors that are associated with it are given elsewhere in this chapter (see p118).

Rock which does not cover (with elevation above MHWS or MHHW or where there is no tide, above MSL).

  (4) (4) (4)

Rock which covers and uncovers (with elevation above chart datum).

    ★ (1₂)
Dries 1.2m   1.2m

Rock awash at the level of chart datum.

Shoal sounding on isolated rock.

 16₅
R   R

Submerged rock not dangerous to surface navigation.

35
R

Submerged danger or obstruction (showing depth cleared by wire drag).

 11₂

Restricted area round the site of a wreck of historical and archaeological importance.

Historic wreck (see note)   Historic wreck (see note)

Coral reef

Covers and uncovers   Always covered

Wreck showing any portion of hull or superstructure at the level of chart datum.

                            Large scale charts

Wreck of which the masts only are visible.

 (Masts)   (Mast 3m)
                                    (Funnel 3m)
                                    (Mast dries 2.1m)

Unsurveyed wreck over which the exact depth is unknown but which is considered to have a safe clearance at the depth shown.

 Wk

Wreck over which the exact depth of water is unknown but is thought to be 28m or less, and which is considered dangerous to surface navigation.

Wreck over which the depth has been obtained by sounding, but not by wire sweep.

 Wk

Wreck which has been swept by wire to the depth shown.

 Wk

Some examples of the symbols used on marine charts to convey essential information in the most concise form.

SYMBOLS AND ABBREVIATIONS

The amount of detail that has to be conveyed on charts can inhibit accurate navigation. To avoid this, symbols and abbreviations are used to reduce clutter, yet still provide important information about each navigational feature.

For example, instead of writing the full details of a light or beacon, it will be abbreviated to: *Gp Fl (3) R ev. 10 sec. 105m 15M*. The navigator will decipher this as a red light 105 metres above sea level, flashing in groups of 3 every 10 seconds and visible for 15 nautical miles.

Symbols are used for the same purpose. For example, navigation lights are marked on a chart with a star to indicate their exact position, and a purple 'flash' is used to indicate that they are suitable for navigational use. All major navigational features are indicated in this way, providing full details of each feature without cluttering up the chart. A special publication can be obtained from chart agents which lists all symbols and abbreviations and their meanings.

NOTICES TO MARINERS

Because details on the chart, such as buoys, may change from time to time, a publication called 'Notices to Mariners' is issued at regular intervals by maritime authorities. It contains full details of any changes relevant to safe navigation, and charts must be regularly updated with this information. The date of the last correction is written in the bottom margin of the chart for future reference.

USEFUL PUBLICATIONS

The following should always be carried on board:

Tide tables: These contain daily tidal movements for all principal ports. A supplementary table gives adjustments for secondary ports.

Sailing Directions and *Pilots:* Sailors' 'guide books', giving detailed information about coastlines, offshore hazards, ports and anything else which may be important for safe navigation. *Pilots* carry more detail of specific areas.

Nautical tables: Standard tables, used for different types of navigation work.

To plot a position: parallel rules are placed against the designated latitude, which is then transposed parallel across the chart at the required location.

A similar action, using the parallel rules against the longitude scale, enables the longitude to be transposed.

A chart table should be big enough to allow charts to be spread out while working.

CHART INSTRUMENTS

Navigators who use a GPS plotter often do not see the need for chart instruments, as their calculations are all done on the screen. To get the best out of an electronic plotter, you should know how to do traditional navigation with paper charts, for which the following are required:

Parallel rules: Sliding rules and roller rules are used to transfer lines parallel across a chart from the working area to the compass rose, or vice versa. The square-shaped Douglas protractor can be used for the same purpose.

Plotters: The popular Breton (or Portland) plotter is a rectangular, transparent plastic device printed or engraved with a square grid. This is lined up with lines of latitude and longitude on the chart to find true north. The straight edge is then lined up with the required bearing, which is read off from the plotter's compass rose.

Dividers: The single-handed variety is the most convenient to use for measuring distances across the chart (see p114).

A pair of compasses: The old school box instruments, these are utilized for drawing circles.

Pencils, erasers: Pencils should be soft (2B grade) so the workings on the chart can be erased without damaging the paper.

A notebook or scrap pad is useful for making notes and jotting down calculations as you work.

A depth sounder is essential when sailing in shallow water, particularly in areas where there are coral reefs, sandbanks or narrow channels.

The log

Although measuring speed is not important in navigation, accurate measurement of distance is vital. The instrument used to record the distance the boat travels through the water is called a log.

The most common type fitted to yachts is operated by a small propeller or a transducer (a type of sensor), which is fitted beneath the hull to electronically measure the speed and distance. The log is activated by the flow of water past the hull, recording the boat's speed and the distance run on a dial in the cockpit.

(Don't confuse the distance log with the log book – the journal in which to record your position, course and details of the passage.)

The depth sounder

Essential for navigation in shallow water areas, the sounder records the depth of water under the hull.

A transducer fitted beneath the hull bounces an electronic pulse off the sea bed and measures the time it takes to echo back to the transducer. The water depth is electronically calculated and indicated on a screen or dial in the cockpit or at the navigator's table.

Some transducers can throw the pulse forwards, providing an early warning of any change in the nature of the sea bed which may affect navigation.

The most useful sounders are those that use a monitor with a full colour display, as they indicate the topography of the sea bed as the boat passes over it, as well as the depth of water under the hull.

These instruments can be so sensitive they will record schools of fish passing under the boat. For this reason, they are sometimes referred to as fish finders.

The old traditional method of measuring depth with a line and sinker is still quite useful for yachts in very shallow waters. The line has a lead weight on the end, which is why it is called the 'lead line' and, when dropped to the bottom, the water depth can be read off from markers on the line as the boat passes over it.

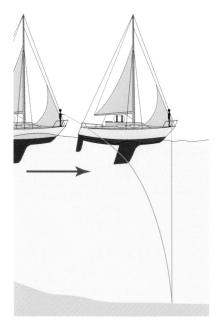

A lead line is a useful way of determining depth when in shallow water.

The marine compass

The principle of the marine compass is similar to that of a boy scout's compass, where a magnetic needle, allowed to swing freely, aligns itself in a north/south direction. The main difference between the two is that the marine compass has a number of magnetic needles attached to the underside of a compass card, so that when the needles swing, the card swings with them, aligning the north point on the card with the magnetic north pole. This makes for easier reading as the card swings more slowly than the needle in a seaway. To, slow things down even more, the compass bowl is filled with a fluid, usually an alcohol mix, which cannot freeze in cold weather.

The earth's magnetic field is best illustrated by the old school experiment of placing a magnet under a sheet of iron filings. The filings align themselves with the lines of magnetic force radiating out of the ends of the magnet (see above).

When a needle is placed in the earth's magnetic field, it similarly aligns itself with the lines of force radiating from the poles. Thus, at any point around the world, a free-swinging compass needle will align itself on a north-south line. The boat can turn in any direction, but the card will always remain pointing in the same direction.

A mark on the compass bowl indicating the centre line of the boat is called a 'lubber line', and

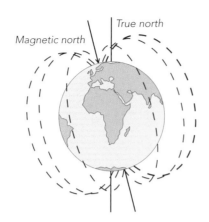

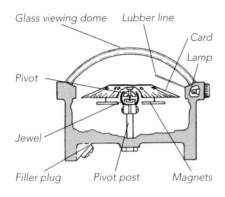

Top left: The earth's magnetic field surrounds the globe. Because magnetic north and true north are not in the same position, a magnetic compass does not point towards true north. The difference between true and magnetic readings is called variation.

Top right: The lines of force running from pole to pole are demonstrated by using a magnet and iron filings.

Left: Inside a typical marine card compass.

the figure on the compass card that is aligned with this mark indicates the compass direction in which the boat is heading. To steer a compass course, the boat is turned until the required heading on the compass card is aligned with the lubber line.

VARIATION

The true north and south poles are not in exactly the same position as the magnetic poles so, since everything on the chart is aligned with the true poles, an error is present in all readings on a magnetic compass. This error is called variation because it varies around the world, but it is well-tabulated

and the error for any specific spot is listed in the centre of the compass rose on the chart for that area. Variation is defined as the deflection of the compass from true north caused by earth's magnetism and it is named east or west.

DEVIATION

Another error that affects the compass reading on board a boat is called deviation. This is caused by the effect on the compass needles of magnetic fittings in the boat itself, such as the steel in the motor, and some electric circuits. In fibreglass and timber boats it is mostly relatively small, but in a steel boat it can be quite considerable.

Deviation can be defined as the deflection of the compass from true north by the boat's magnetism, and it is also named east or west.

Deviation changes according to the direction in which the boat is heading, so it must be taken into account each time the boat alters course. To find the deviation, the boat is taken out into open water and swung round through all points of the compass. Compass readings taken on each heading are compared with true bearings from the chart and the difference between them is tabulated and listed on what is called a Deviation Card (a typical example is shown below). A quick reference to this card indicates the deviation for any course on which the boat might head and is applied to all compass readings.

To reduce the swing of the card and make steering easier, most master compasses consist of a globe or dome filled with a fluid that dampens any severe movement, as well as allowing the compass card to remain level when the boat heels.

THE MASTER COMPASS

Deviation can sometimes be removed or reduced by a professional compass adjuster, who places correcting magnets around the main or master compass in the cockpit. As its name denotes, this is the principal compass in the boat and is therefore the one that is checked regularly to ensure deviation is remaining constant. It is usually the steering compass and is located in the cockpit close to the wheel or tiller.

THE HAND-BEARING COMPASS

This is a smaller compass used for taking bearings of shore objects for plotting the boat's position. There are many different types, but all have the common characteristic of being portable so that bearings can be taken from anywhere around the boat where there is clear line of sight on shore objects. The hand-bearing compass is not corrected for deviation, so must be compared with the master compass from the point where it is being used, as the deviation may differ at points around the boat. It is usually held at eye level and a sighting device used to line up the shore objects before a reading is taken (see p124).

DEVIATION CARD
Vessel: Carousel

Boat's head		Deviation
N	000	0
NE	045	2E
E	090	4E
SE	135	2E
S	180	0
SW	225	2W
W	270	4W
NW	315	2W
N	360	0

A typical small boat deviation card.

COMPASS ERROR

Since every reading on a compass contains errors in both variation and deviation, the readings must be corrected before being used for navigation. The two errors are combined to form what is known as compass error by simply adding like names or subtracting unlike names as follows:

> *Variation 5° E*
> + *Deviation 2° E*
> = *compass error 7° E*

> *Variation 5° E*
> − *Deviation 2° W*
> = *compass error 3° E*

Basically, this means that when different names are given to items in navigation (N and S; E and W), you add the like names (E and E) and subtract the unlike names.

Every reading on the magnetic compass has this error, so it must be corrected before being used for navigational work on a chart, which uses only true readings.

A course laid off on the chart is true (no errors), so it must be converted to a compass course before it can be used for steering the boat.

Similarly, a bearing of a shore object taken on the hand-bearing compass must be converted to true before it can be laid off on the chart. The conversion process can get somewhat confusing, but a little memory aid used for centuries by mariners, will help:

> *If the error is east,*
> *the compass is least.*
> *If the error is west,*
> *the compass is best.*

> *If the error is east*, the compass reading (C) is least (or less than) the true (T) reading.
> *If the error is west*, the compass reading (C) is better than the true (T) reading.

A couple of practical examples might make this clearer:

(i) A course from point A to point B is laid off on a chart and reads 266°T (True) when read off the adjacent compass rose. The compass error is 5°E. (As error east = compass least, the compass course must be less than the true course.) The boat must therefore steer 261°C (compass reading) in order to follow the course of 266°T (true reading) on the chart.

(ii) A bearing on a shore object, taken with a hand bearing compass, reads 266°C. The compass error is 5°W. Error west = compass best, so the true bearing to be laid on the chart must be less than the compass bearing. The bearing laid on the chart will be 261°T.

ELECTRONIC COMPASSES

Although most yachts still use the traditional magnetic compass, larger ocean-going craft prefer electronic compasses.

These come in a number of forms; the gyro compass, fluxgate compass and laser ring compass. Gyro and laser compasses are very expensive and are rarely encountered on family yachts, but one of their advantages is that they are not subject to compass error, which means that the reading on the compass is true, the same as the chart.

The less expensive fluxgate, or digital, compass is favoured by many yachtsmen, especially those on ocean passages. It eliminates, or at least reduces, deviation and its digital read-out is far easier to follow than that of a swinging magnetic compass card. It can also be interfaced with the autopilot and wind instruments.

The coastal passage

A coastal passage between two ports must be carefully planned beforehand if the boat is to make the best possible track consistent with safety. The shortest track is a straight line between the ports, but this is rarely possible, since offshore hazards or dangers can get in the way. To overcome this, a composite course is laid down, consisting of shorter straight lines which circumnavigate the dangers.

As described earlier, navigation within a harbour is mostly visual, using buoys and beacons to follow the channels out through the entrance. Once in open water, the coastal passage begins at a predetermined departure position. From here, the navigator starts to plot the composite courses to an arrival position off the next port. The procedure for laying off the courses is as follows:

1. Determine the first hazard or danger that will be encountered along the passage, and assess a safe distance for the boat to pass. With a pair of compasses set at this safe distance and the point of the compasses on the outer edge of the hazard, draw a circle to seaward around it. This is known as a danger circle.

2. Draw the first course from the departure point as a tangent to the danger circle. Transfer this line to the nearest compass rose and read off the true heading for the first course. Apply compass error (as described on p120) to obtain the compass course to steer on the first leg.

3. Determine the next danger and draw a danger circle around it as before, then use the parallel rules to join the two circles with a line at a tangent to both. This is the second true course and must be converted to a compass course to steer, as on the first leg.

4. Continue with this procedure, circumnavigating all the dangers between the departure and arrival positions until the last hazard is reached. The final course will be a tangent from the last danger circle to the arrival position off the destination.

5. A boat following these courses will make the shortest passage between departure and arrival points, clearing all dangers by the pre-determined safe distance. If the boat sailed along each course line without drifting to one side or the other, life for the navigator would be easy. But there are a number of factors that affect the boat's progress and, unless these are taken into account, it will be pushed off course with the risk of drifting into danger.

Two of the major culprits are current effect and leeway (see p122). Current effect is the tendency of ocean currents or tidal flows to push the boat off course, while leeway has the same effect but is caused by the wind.

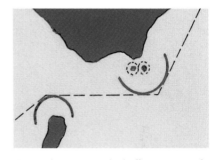

A complex course is laid off as a series of tangents to danger circles, which indicate rocks or other offshore hazards.

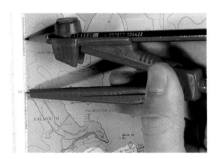

To create a danger circle, a compass is set at the safe distance, measured from the latitude scale at the edge of the chart.

From the outermost point of the danger, a circle is drawn around it. The yacht must not sail inside this circle.

CURRENTS

Ocean currents are fairly pre-dictable well offshore, but close to the coast there is a tendency for stray counter-currents and back eddies to swirl around headlands and in and out of bays. Tidal streams can be predicted for har-bours and estuaries but, in the open waters along the coast, they are influenced by topographical features and are often quite irreg-ular. These can combine to create an unpredictable factor which can push a boat off its steered course.

LEEWAY

The forward movement of a boat results from the wind pushing on one side and the keel countering from the other (see p14). However, the balance between these two factors is never quite even, and there is a tendency for the boat to slip sideways through the water despite the effect of the keel's lat-eral resistance.

This is known as leeway and it obviously varies from boat to boat according to the underwater pro-file as well as the sailing position. It is at a maximum when the boat is hard on the wind and is heeled well over, but is negligible when it is upright and running before the wind. Leeway can be quite consid-erable, pushing a boat off course by as much as 10–15 degrees, so it must be taken into account when setting the course. It is always allowed into the wind.

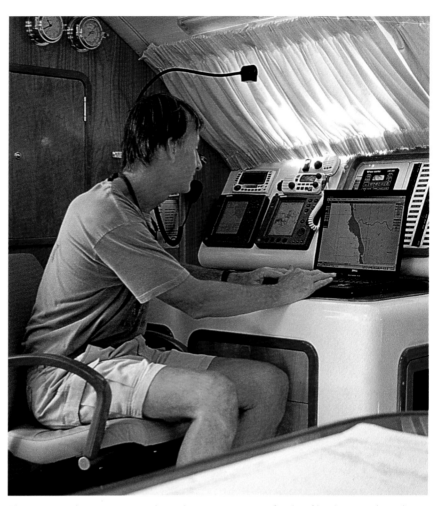

Plotting co-ordinates is essential on a long passage out of sight of land, as it is the only way to keep track of your position on the ocean.

Plotting co-ordinates

While on a passage, it is often important to know the boat's lati-tude and longitude. Apart from keeping a progress report in the boat's log book, if an emergency does occur, the boat's location must be reported to a shore sta-tion or rescue organization.

It is sometimes necessary to plot a position from given latitude and longitude co-ordinates, such as when locating a navigation hazard or a vessel in distress.

There are a number of ways to plot co-ordinates, but the method described below is the most basic.

When taking the boat's position from a chart, the parallel rules are aligned with the nearest parallel of latitude and then moved up to intersect with the boat's position. The latitude of that position can be read off where the rules touch the latitude scale on the side of the chart. The dividers are placed along the edge of the rules with one point on the boat's position

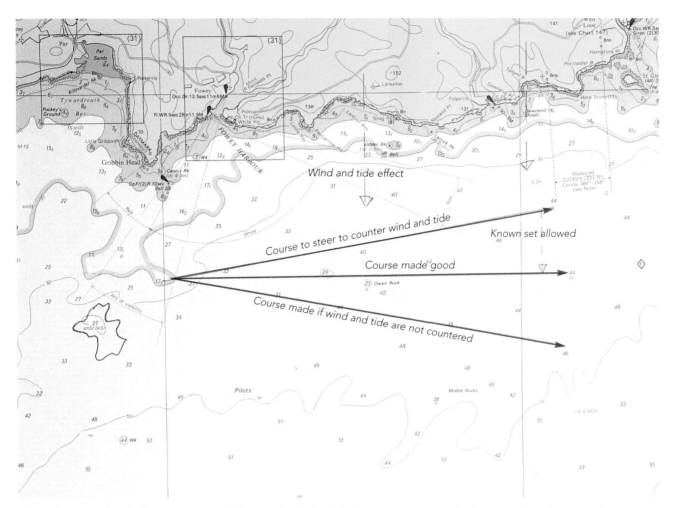

Wind and tide effect

Course to steer to counter wind and tide

Known set allowed

Course made good

Course made if wind and tide are not countered

'Set' is the amount by which a boat is pushed off course by wind and tidal movement. Set may be known, such as where a tidal effect can be determined from tables, for instance; or unknown, such as variable wind speeds (see p129).

and the other on the nearest meridian of longitude. By transferring the dividers to the longitude scale at the top or bottom of the chart, the longitude can be read.

To plot a position, the procedure is reversed. The parallel rules are aligned with the nearest parallel of latitude on the side scale, then moved up or down to the required latitude reading. A pencil-line drawn along the rules at this point marks the required latitude on the chart. The dividers are placed on the longitude scale with one point on the nearest meridian and the other on the required longitude. They are then transferred down the chart to the same meridian and the longitude is measured off along the latitude line.

FIXING THE BOAT'S POSITION

When a boat begins its passage along the first course line, it is unlikely to follow it exactly, as factors such as tides, currents, wind and wave effects, can cause it to drift off course. Since many of these factors are unknown, they cannot be applied beforehand. However, it is important that their effect on the boat is monitored by checking its position frequently and entering the results on the chart.

This is known as plotting and is usually carried out at hourly intervals, although the timing can vary according to the weather and sea conditions, the distance offshore, and the number of visible objects available for plotting.

The hand-bearing compass is a used when making coastal passages, as it can be carried around the boat until a position is found with good sight of the shoreline.

COMPASS BEARINGS

On small-boats in coastal waters, plotting is usually carried out with a hand-bearing compass, using shore objects as reference points.

Lighthouses, tall buildings and prominent headlands are ideal for plotting; hills and low shore-lines are not. The object used must have a clear-cut edge or tip to provide an accurate compass bearing and must be positively identified on the chart.

A bearing is taken by aligning a hand-bearing compass with the object and reading off the bearing. The reading must then be corrected for compass error before laying off the bearing on the chart.

The procedure for laying off a bearing on the chart is much the same as that for laying off a course line (see p121), but this time in reverse. The parallel rules are set on the nearest compass rose so that one edge bisects the centre. Where that same edge bisects the outer ring of the compass rose, the true bearing is read off.

The parallel rules are then carefully moved across the chart until one edge touches the object used for the bearing. A pencil line drawn along the edge of the parallel rules, from the shore object to seaward, gives the bearing of the object. The position of the boat lies somewhere along that line.

Estimated position

If conditions are good and the boat's position can be plotted satisfactorily, the passage should be easy. However, if conditions are such that the position cannot be checked regularly with shore objects, an estimated position (EP) will be all that is available.

By using all recorded information on the boat's progress along the course line, such as the course steered, the distance run by log, estimated leeway and tide and any other known factors, an EP can be found. This is obviously not completely accurate, but the best that can be obtained under the circumstances. Draw a triangle to indicate that it is an estimated position.

If you use only the course steered and distance travelled, you will get a dead reckoning (DR) position (derived from the term 'deduced reckoning'), but this is less accurate over a longer distance.

Cross bearing fix

One of the easiest and most accurate methods of plotting the boat's position is a cross bearing fix. This requires at least two (preferably three) shore objects to be visible, and the bearings must be taken at the same time. The objects should be spaced around 30–45° apart for the most accurate angle between the bearings and thus the best chances of an accurate fix. Once taken, the bearings must be converted to true bearings.

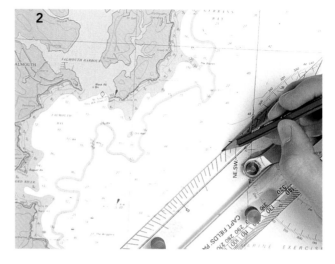

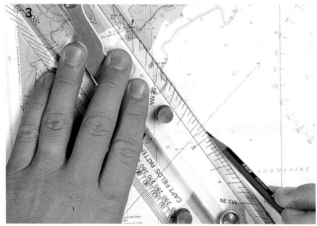

MAKING A CROSS BEARING FIX

A single bearing line drawn on a chart from a shore object indicates that the boat's position lies somewhere along that line, but not exactly where (1). The point at which the bearing cuts the course line is where the navigator would like to be (2) but if the boat has drifted inshore or offshore, a single bearing will give no indication of how far it may have drifted. A second bearing, taken from another shore object at the same time as the first, should cross the first bearing, giving a better indication of the boat's position (3). In practice, most navigators use three bearings to eliminate any possibility of error (4). Where the three bearings cross is a positive indication of the boat's position and a circle is drawn around it to indicate that it is a fix (5). The final position is likely to be a 'cocked hat', as the boat is moving.

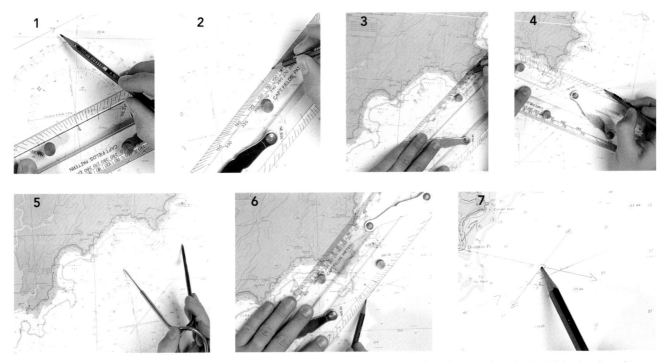

A running fix enables you to plot your course continuously along a coastline at night, or when there are few clearly visible shoreline objects.

Running fixes

It is often difficult, sometimes impossible, to get three shore objects in view at the same time. Indeed, getting two good objects can be a problem, and a common situation, when making a passage well offshore, is that only one worthwhile object is visible.

In this case a procedure known as a running fix is employed to establish the boat's position. While it is not as accurate as a cross-bearing fix, over a number of fixes it can provide a fairly accurate indication of how the boat is progressing and where it is in relation to the course line. A running fix involves the use of the distance log as well as the hand-bearing compass.

MAKING A RUNNING FIX

A bearing is taken of a shore object when it is well ahead, and the log-reading noted. The bearing is laid off on the chart, as before; where it crosses the course line is an estimate of the boat's position (1). This is a slightly better estimate than a DR, because the boat's position must be somewhere along the bearing, hopefully where it crosses the course line.

The boat continues along its course until the bearing of the shore object has widened by about 30°, when a second bearing is taken and laid off on the chart together with the log reading (2).

The log distance run between bearings is measured along the course line from the first bearing to a point we shall call X. The first bearing is then transferred parallel to point X, and marked off on the chart (3–6). Where the transferred first bearing cuts the second bearing is the fix of the boat's position, which is circled (7).

As unknown factors may have affected the boat during the run from first to second bearing, the procedure is repeated using the second bearing as the first and running it forward to a third bearing, taken when the shore object has opened out a further 30°.

This is repeated when another 30° has passed and the boat is abeam of the object. The running fixes made to this point will indicate how the boat is progressing in relation to the course line.

RUNNING FIX BETWEEN TWO OBJECTS

When there are few suitable shore objects visible, or at night, when running between lighthouses, a series of running fixes using one object can be continued along the boat's track by using another object up ahead.

As the first object starts to fall astern, a bearing can be taken of the next object up ahead, and the last bearing of the first object is transferred forward and crossed with the first bearing of the next object. The procedure is the same as for a running fix from an single object, so the boat's position is where the transferred first bearing cuts the second bearing. Circle it and note the time and log reading.

With a series of shore objects conveniently spaced along the coastline, the fixes can be continued indefinitely, giving a good check on the boat's progress.

Doubling the angle on the bow fix: because only two bearings are used, a single fix cannot be relied on, thus a series of fixes is made to establish the boat's position and progress.

OTHER RUNNING FIXES

Another fix that uses the same principle as the running fix is known as 'doubling the angle on the bow'. A bearing is taken when the object is fine on the bow and the log noted, as well as the relative angle between the bearing and the course line. This bearing is converted to true and laid off on the chart, just as for a normal running fix. The boat continues on its course until the relative angle has doubled, when another bearing and log reading is taken.

When laid off on the chart, an isosceles triangle (with two equal sides) will be drawn, indicating that the distance run by log between the bearings is the distance of the boat off the object on the second bearing. The fix can be repeated when the relative angle has doubled again.

The 'four-point bearing fix' is similar but involves only two bearings; the first when the object is at 45° to the course line and the second when it is abeam. This again creates an isosceles triangle in

which the distance run by log between the two bearings is equal to the distance offshore on the second bearing. Since the second bearing is also the beam bearing, this provides a convenient regular check on the boat's position without the use of the compass.

The four-point bearing and beam bearing can be judged by eye, using part of the boat (such as a shroud) as the four point and beam bearing indicators respectively.

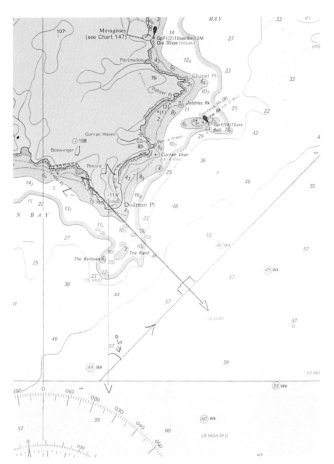

Four-point bearing fix: As there are eight points of the compass between the bow and the beam of the boat (90°), the four-point bearing is at 45° to the bow.

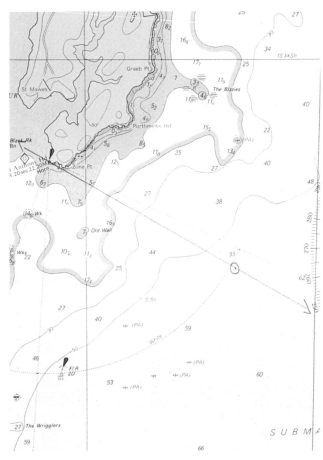

When navigating well offshore, or making a landfall after an ocean crossing, the extreme range fix is often the only means of establishing the boat's position.

Extreme range fix

This is a handy fix when making along a coastline at night where there are few lighthouses to provide fixes. It involves the use of a phenomenon known as the 'break' of the light. When the light from an ocean lighthouse is first seen it is usually below the horizon, and all that is visible is the 'loom' of the rotating beams of light sweeping the sky, rather like those of a searchlight. By watching the loom, it is possible to identify the lighthouse from the chart (see p110).

At the moment the light comes over the horizon, it 'breaks' and the loom disappears, replaced by a distinct, bright flash.

The distance, or range, at which the transition from flash to loom takes place is called the 'rising' or 'dipping' distance, depending on whether the light is appearing or disappearing over the horizon.

A bearing is taken at the moment the light breaks, and laid off on the chart. From the Extreme Range tables (also known as the dipping tables) provided with any set of nautical tables, and using the height (elevation) of the lighthouse taken from the chart, and the height of the eye of the observer on the boat, the distance from the light can be obtained and laid off along the bearing to obtain an accurate fix of the boat's position.

This is a useful fix when making landfall after a passage over an open sea, as it allows the navigator to adjust course while still well away from land, but it does require both a powerful light and a clear night sky.

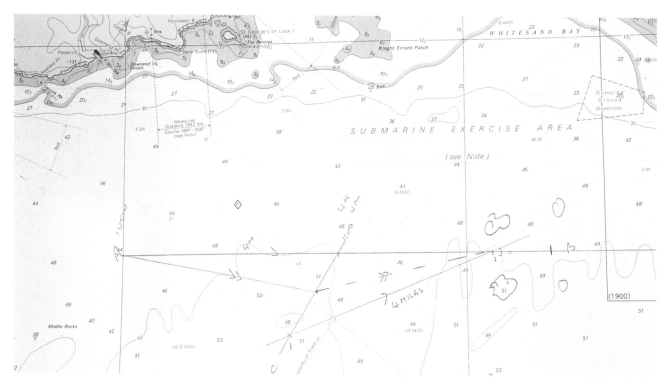

Unknown factors that push the boat off course cannot be counteracted until their effect is known. The difference between the course steered and the course made good over a period of time is the amount the boat is being set off course. When this has been found, it is then applied in order to achieve the required course.

The unknown set

No matter how careful the steering or how accurate the navigation, the boat will almost certainly wander off course at some stage. This is the result of unknown factors (such as winds or tides) for which no allowance could be made when commencing the passage.

However, when a series of fixes indicate just how much and in what direction the boat has drifted, steps can be taken to correct the problem and make allowances for it on the remaining passage.

A line drawn from the departure position through the fixes made during the first leg of the passage will indicate both the direction and the distance the boat has actually travelled. This is called the Course Made Good (CMG). By reading this course off the compass rose, the difference between the course steered and the CMG can be determined. This is the amount by which the boat has been affected by the 'unknown set'. By applying it to the course in the opposite direction, the unknown set can be counteracted.

Unfortunately, this set rarely remains the same for very long so, in order to keep the boat as close as possible to its required course, the exercise will need to be carried out at regular intervals throughout the passage.

After a long passage at sea, it is always reassuring when your navigation takes you to where you want to be.

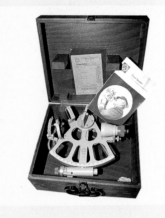  

OCEAN NAVIGATION

In many ways, celestial (ocean) and coastal navigation are similar. Both use charts, both use instruments for plotting the boat's position and both use somewhat similar methods of obtaining fixes. The main difference is that coastal navigation uses land objects to establish the boat's position, while celestial navigation uses heavenly bodies. Of course, there are other differences in practice; coastal navigation involves very little calculation, whereas celestial navigation involves quite complex calculations, and celestial sight-taking is restricted to certain hours of the day, whereas coastal fixes can be taken day or night. GPS is common to both and used in much the same way for ocean navigation as it is for coastal work. But, as mentioned before, GPS can be subject to problems which are not always easily fixed in the middle of an ocean. For this reason, the sextant and the traditional methods of calculating celestial sights are still an important part of navigation on the open seas.

Charts were once painstakingly drawn by hand; nowadays, satellites play a role in mapping every inch of the earth's surface.

Charts for ocean passages

When making an open ocean or long coastal voyage, it is necessary to carry a number of charts. Large-scale charts of the departure and arrival ports are essential, as are charts of any ports the boat may visit. Smart sailors include charts of ports along the planned track, and which may become a port of call in an emergency.

Medium-scale charts, covering the coastlines you will encounter at the beginning and end of the passage, are vital, as are charts of coastal areas that may be passed en route. You will also need at least one small-scale chart covering the main area of ocean to be crossed, on which you can plot the boat's track progressively.

Ocean current charts (see p139) are useful for planning routes that avoid adverse currents, and charts of global wind patterns at different times of the year are also useful.

All of the above are standard charts which can be obtained from a good chart agent. Before leaving port, all charts must be updated with the latest Notices to Mariners.

For ocean passages, especially in higher latitudes, a gnomonic chart will save a lot of unnecessary sailing. A straight line drawn on a gnomonic chart is a straight line on the earth's surface and therefore the shortest track from one point to another on the globe (see p141).

Electronic charts are available as CDs or cartridges. When interfaced with GPS, way points and courses can be calculated without the need for a gnomonic chart. Electronic charts usually give the option of plotting a rhumb line or great circle course.

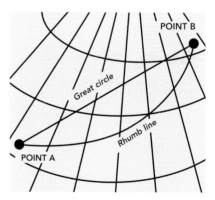

On a gnomonic chart, the great circle route appears straight.

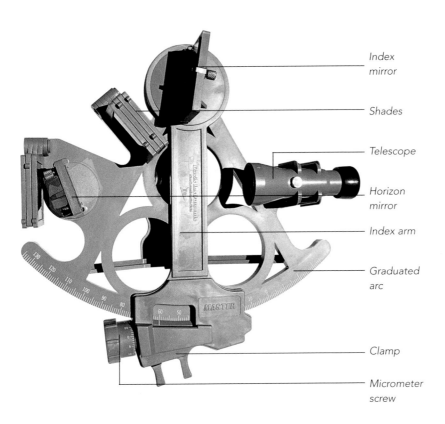

Index mirror

Shades

Telescope

Horizon mirror

Index arm

Graduated arc

Clamp

Micrometer screw

Above: The principle of the sextant has remained unchanged since it was invented by Sir Isaac Newton in the 18th century, and it is still a key tool for all celestial navigators.

Below: To take a reading with a sextant, the angle of the sun above the horizon (the altitude) is found by sighting the sun and horizon through the telescope. When they are in alignment, the altitude is read off the arc.

The sextant

The main instrument for traditional ocean navigation, the sextant measures the angle of the sun (or the stars, the planets or the moon) above the horizon. By means of two mirrors, and using the split image principle of a camera rangefinder, the sextant 'lowers' the sun in one mirror down to the horizon, which is seen in the other mirror, and measures the angle on a scale on the sextant's arc.

The index mirror, the moving part of the sextant, is attached to the index arm. The sun is reflected from this mirror, through shades that reduce it to a visible disk, into the horizon mirror, which is vertically divided in half, with the outside half consisting of clear glass.

The sun is brought down into the mirrored half and adjusted by means of the micrometer screw until it 'sits' on the horizon, as seen through the clear glass.

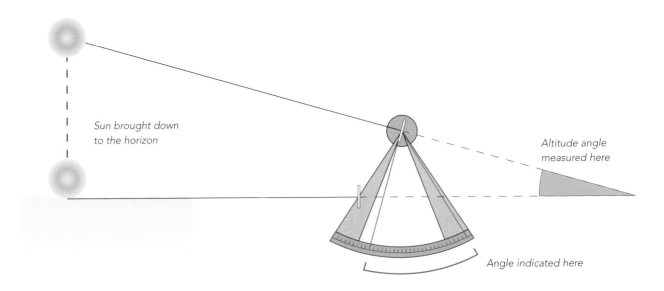

Sun brought down to the horizon

Altitude angle measured here

Angle indicated here

Index error: when the sextant is set at zero, the true and reflected horizons should form an unbroken line. If they do not (as depicted above), then index error is present.

Side error: If the horizon separates when the sextant is tilted to one side (as depicted above), then side error is present.

Correcting the sextant

The mirrors are a vital, and delicate, part of the sextant, and can be put out of alignment by the slightest bump; even by heat and humidity. If they are damaged or dislodged from their correct position, errors will occur in the readings.

To ensure that the mirrors are correctly aligned, it is important to run a quick check on them each day before taking the first sight. The principle errors and the method of checking them are as follows:

INDEX ERROR

This occurs when the faces of the two mirrors are not parallel. It is found by setting the sextant at absolute zero and sighting through the telescope at the horizon. Since it is not measuring any angle, both reflected and true horizons should appear in a straight line. If this is the case, there is no index error, but if they are out of alignment, index error exists.

By adjusting the micrometer screw until both horizons are correctly aligned, the amount of index error can be read off the scale and applied to all sextant readings. Unless it is large, this error is rarely taken out by adjusting the mirrors, it is just recorded and applied to the sextant readings. It can be found at night by using a star instead of the horizon.

SIDE ERROR

This occurs when the horizon mirror is not perpendicular to the body of the sextant. It is found by setting the sextant at absolute zero again, and looking at the horizon through the telescope. The sextant is then tilted sideways until it is at an angle of about 45°.

If the true and reflected horizons have moved out of alignment, side error is present and must be removed by adjusting the small screw on the back of the horizon mirror farthest from the frame of the instrument.

PERPENDICULARITY

This is a difficult error to check. It is caused by the index mirror not being perpendicular to the frame of the instrument. To find it, the sextant must be turned around until the arc can be seen reflected in the index mirror by looking down at an oblique angle from above. If the reflected arc seen in the mirror is in alignment with the true arc seen beyond the mirror, perpendicularity does not exist. If the arcs are out of alignment, the error must be removed by turning the small screw on the back of the index mirror.

Using the sextant

Once the sextant has been checked for errors, it is ready to measure the angle of the sun (or another celestial body) above the horizon.

Just looking through the telescope at the horizon and trying to bring the sun down by adjusting the arc can be rather frustrating. A widely used method is to set the sextant at 0, pull all shades into place, then point the instrument directly at the sun. Two suns will be seen, one true and one reflected. By slowly lowering the sextant, and at the same time adjusting the index arm to hold the reflected sun in the mirror, the sun can be brought down until the horizon appears in the clear glass of the horizon mirror. From there, it is a simple matter of fine adjustment to prepare the sextant for sight-taking.

Most sextant readings are done using the sun, but the procedure for sight-taking with the moon, planets or stars is identical although, of course, shades are not required.

The angle of the sun above the horizon can only be accurate when it is taken with the sextant held absolutely vertical. If the sextant is tilted out of the vertical, it will give an incorrect reading.

To ensure the sextant is plumb, it is rocked from side to side, causing the image of the sun to rise and fall as it sweeps across the horizon (in much the same way as the bubble in a spirit level); when the sun is at the lowest point of its curve, the sextant is vertical and the sight can be taken. It is essential to rock the sextant if you are to obtain a true altitude reading.

TIMING

Time plays a very important part in celestial navigation. Basically, the boat's position is found by relating it to the position of the sun (or another body) at the time the sight was taken. The position of all celestial bodies for every hour, minute and second of every day can be found in the *Nautical Almanac*, so the precise timing of the sight is essential if the boat's position is to be calculated accurately.

In the days before radio, when ships were at sea for months without any contact with the shore, extremely accurate chronometers

A good wrist watch set on UT (universal time) is all that is needed for sights, provided it is checked with radio signals before sight-taking.

and a final star sight at dusk. Sights cannot be taken during the night due to the lack of a visible horizon.

TAKING THE SIGHTS

Sight-taking is the same for sun, moon, planets or stars, the only difference being that with sun, the lower limb (bottom edge) is always landed on the horizon. On yachts and small craft, the moon is not used much because both the sights and calculations are much more involved than with other bodies. Stars and planets too, can be difficult to hold in the sextant when the boat is moving in a seaway, so the sun is the mainstay of sight-taking on boats. The details given here are for the sun.

When a sight is to be taken, the sun is brought down to the horizon in the horizon mirror as described earlier. Because it is rising or falling, except at noon, adjustment with the micrometer screw is necessary to hold it on the horizon.

At the precise moment the sight is taken, the time is recorded to the nearest second by an assistant with a watch. Most navigators take at least two sights to reduce the chance of error in either the sextant reading or the time.

The noon sight is taken as the sun crosses the meridian, which means it will rise, then peak and start falling. The moment of crossing the meridian, when it peaks, is the reading that is used for the noon latitude sight calculation.

(timepieces) were carried, but today, radio time signals can be obtained just prior to sight taking, and a good wristwatch is then sufficient for the timing of the sights.

Time signals can be obtained in a number of ways. Radio stations broadcast frequent time checks that can be picked up by vessels at sea. Two official publications, the *Admiralty List of Radio Signals* (UK) and *Radio Navigational Aids* (US), carry detailed information about world radio stations and their frequencies. In navigation, Universal Time (UT), formerly Greenwich Mean Time (GMT), is used.

The navigator's day

In order to monitor progress across an ocean, many navigators follow a routine where, provided weather conditions permit, the boat's position is checked frequently by celestial sights – sometimes up to five times a day. A morning sight, using three or four stars, is taken at dawn when it is light enough for the horizon to be seen clearly, but dark enough for the stars to still be visible. The sun is used for the next sight, taken soon after breakfast, and a noon sight when the sun crosses the meridian. Another sun sight is taken mid to late afternoon,

The computations

There are a number of ways that sight calculations can be worked, but the easiest for small boat navigators is the Sight Reduction method. Two volumes of tables are required for this computation; the *Nautical Almanac* and the *Sight Reduction Tables*, which can be obtained from any nautical bookshop. The *Nautical Almanac* lists the position in the heavens of the sun, moon, planets and stars for every second of every day. As the name denotes, the *Sight Reduction Tables* is a volume of tables used for the sight computation.

There is no room in a book of this nature to cover these complex computations in detail, so the description is confined to the most basic, but nevertheless accurate, of the sight-taking computations: that of the latitude by meridian altitude, or the noon sight (see p138).

ALTITUDE CORRECTION

The angle of the sun above the horizon is known as the altitude, and it is the first requirement for commencing the sight calculation. Apart from errors in the mirrors, which have already been dealt with, there are a number of other errors in the altitude-reading which must also be adjusted before it can be used.

Corrections for these errors, which are mostly concerned with the earth's atmosphere, the size of the sun, the horizon, and other

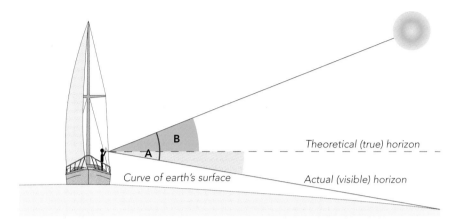

Dip is the result of landing the sun (in the sextant) on the false horizon created by the curvature of the earth (A). The true horizon is at eye level (B). The correction for the curve is the dip.

Deflection of the sun's image through atmospheric refraction is one factor in the correction of altitude.

non-sextant factors, are listed in the *Nautical Almanac* in two tables, often located on the inside covers or on a convenient separate card.

One table deals with Dip, which is an error created by the earth's surface being curved, and the other is the Altitude Correction Table, which provides a single correction factor for all other errors.

THE CELESTIAL SPHERE

All heavenly bodies are located on an imaginary celestial sphere surrounding the earth. An identical grid to earth's latitude and longitude is used to locate the positions of the stars and planets. On the celestial sphere, latitude is termed declination (dec) and longitude the Greenwich Hour Angle (GHA).

Declination is exactly the same as latitude, running 90° north and south from the celestial equator to the poles but, unlike longitude, which runs 180° east and west, the GHA runs 360° right around the globe westward from the prime meridian. Thus the equivalent of a longitude of 90°W on earth would be 90°GHA on the celestial globe, but the equivalent of 90° east longitude would be 270°GHA.

When the sun is right overhead at noon (meridian passage) it will have a GHA the same as the boat's longitude (W).

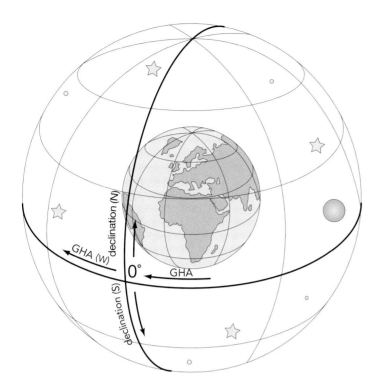

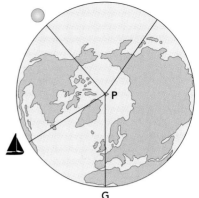

Greenwich Hour Angle (GHA)

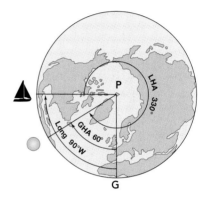

The celestial sphere is effectively just an extension of the earth's globe in space. Declination and GHA are the equivalent of earth's latitude and longitude, although GHA is measured 360° west and longitude 2 x 180° west or east.

The relationship between Local Hour Angle, GHA and Longitude. LHA can be either 30°E or 330°W.

LOCAL-HOUR ANGLE AND LONGITUDE

An hour angle is the number of degrees and minutes between two meridians. Thus GHA is the angle between the prime meridian and the sun measured westward.

Local-hour angle (LHA) is the angle between any two meridians (the boat and the sun, for example) and can be measured east or west. If, say, the boat is on the meridian of longitude 90°W, and the sun is rising with a GHA of 60°, the LHA must be 30°E.

This gives rise to a formula which is used widely in navigation:
Longitude = GHA + or – LHA.

In theory this can be put to immediate use to find a boat's position.

The exact time is taken when the sun crosses the boat's meridian and is checked against the *Nautical Almanac*, which lists the position of the sun for every second of every day. Against the time (GMT) of meridian altitude, the sun's GHA can be extracted and the boat's longitude found as follows:
Longitude = GHA + or – LHA.
Since there is no LHA (because the sun is on the meridian), therefore
Longitude = GHA.

This is not the usual way of finding the longitude at noon, as obtaining the exact second when the sun crosses the meridian can be difficult to pinpoint, but it gives an approximate longitude which

can be crossed with the latitude by meridian passage to indicate the boat's progress (see p138).

Precise accuracy in celestial work is often not possible on small craft due to the difficulties of taking a sextant sight in any sort of a seaway. However, it does provide a basic fix at the time the sun crosses the meridian, and that is better than relying on DR (see p124). A widely practised and more accurate method is to cross the latitude reading with a longitude-by-sight reduction transferred from the morning sights, but that is beyond the scope of this book.

THE NOON SIGHT (LATITUDE BY MERIDIAN PASSAGE)

The secret of accuracy with this sight is to ensure that it is taken at the exact moment the sun peaks in the sextant mirrors, because that is the precise moment it reaches its zenith. It takes two people to achieve this accurately; one to take the exact time, the other to stay glued to the sextant telescope.

As the sun rises, it will appear to move up off the horizon in the sextant then, as it approaches the meridian passage, will slow and momentarily stop before starting to fall again. While obtaining the maximum altitude in the sextant is easy, picking the exact time when the sun reaches its zenith is the hard part.

OTHER SIGHTS AND COMPUTATIONS

The latitude by meridian passage described opposite is the simplest of the celestial sight computations, but there are many other methods of taking and computing sextant sights using the sun, as well as more complex sights using stars, planets and the moon.

The 'navigator's day' (see p135) indicates the use of a number of different sights during the course of one day at sea, the meridian passage (noon sight) providing a latitude, morning and afternoon sun sights both producing a longitude, and star sights calculated to resolution with a full latitude and longitude fix.

To determine latitude by meridian passage (the noon sight), the latitude is calculated from the sextant altitude as follows:

1. Correct the sextant altitude for any index error. The result will be the observed altitude (obs alt).

2. Subtract the dip correction (dip) from the *Nautical Almanac* to obtain the apparent altitude (app alt).

3. Locate the altitude correction (alt corr) in the *Nautical Almanac* and apply it to find True Altitude (true alt/Ho).

4. Subtract true altitude (Ho) from 90° to find ZX (the zenith distance). If the sun is to the north, ZX is south (i.e. the boat is to the south of the sun), and vice versa.

5. From the *Nautical Almanac* extract the sun's declination (dec) for the time of the sight and apply it to the ZX (add like names, subtract unlike.)

6. The result is an accurate latitude which can be plotted on the chart and crossed with the longitude obtained earlier (see p137) for a reasonable fix of the boat's position.

DR (dead reckoning):	Lat 35° 17' S Long 151° 01' E
UT (universal time/GMT):	02h 04m 10s
Date:	15 December 2001
Noon Sext Alt	77° 42.0'
Index error	01.0' −
Obs Alt	77° 41.0'
Dip	03.0' −
App Alt	77° 38.0'
Alt Corr	16.0' +
True Alt (Ho)	77° 54.0'
	90° 00.0'
True Alt (Ho)	77° 54.0' −
ZX (Zenith distance)	12° 06.0'
Sun's dec	23° 15.7' S +
NOON LATITUDE	35° 21.7' S

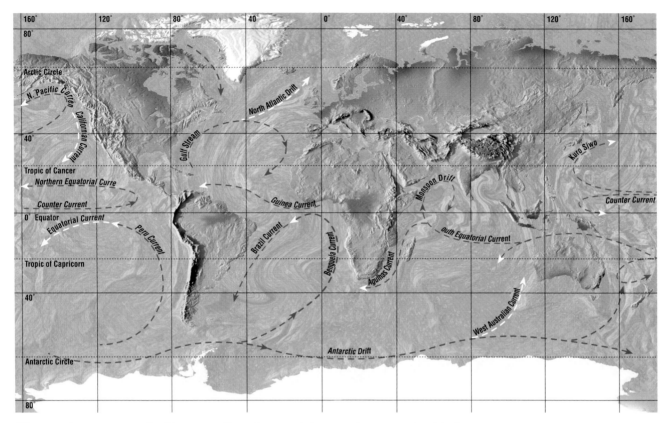

When crossing oceans, you should try to use the major currents to your advantage and avoid adverse currents.

Crossing the oceans

In planning a passage across an open ocean, a number of factors need to be considered. Apart from obvious things, such as ensuring you have sufficient supplies of food and water and that the boat has been prepared for potentially hazardous sea conditions, the navigation side of the trip will require a different approach to coastal or inshore passages.

The use of the sextant to fix the boat's position at regular intervals has already been dealt with, but aspects such as ocean currents, prevailing wind systems, and the curvature of the earth's surface, also come into play.

OCEAN CURRENTS

Around the edge of each major ocean, currents run in a mainly anti-clockwise direction (southern hemisphere) and clockwise direction (northern hemisphere) . There are a few exceptions, but the general trend follows this pattern.

These currents are quite strong in places. For example, when the Agulhas current, off the east coast of South Africa, is running strongly, it can sometimes be almost impossible for a sailboat to stem. The Equatorial current, running across the tropical regions, can push a boat way off course when it loses wind in the doldrums, while the Gulf Stream, well known as the

lifeblood of Northern Europe, creates a massive movement of warm water across the North Atlantic towards what would otherwise be the frozen north.

Strong currents have a marked influence on low-powered boats such as yachts and, since their effect can be either beneficial or quite disastrous, currents must be taken into consideration when planning a passage.

Current charts are most useful when preparing an ocean crossing, as they can indicate how to take advantage of some currents and avoid others. Sometimes a sizable detour might be necessary to pick up a favourable current or avoid

Trade winds are prevailing winds that blow toward the equator from the northeast and southeast. They are caused by hot air rising at the equator and the consequent inward movement of air from north and south to take its place. The doldrums, an area of unpredictable calms, lie at their convergence. Winds are deflected to the west because of the earth's west to east rotation. The trade wind belts move about five degrees to the north and south with the seasons.

one that will head the boat. Since some open ocean currents can run at speeds of up to five knots they must be avoided by yachts that might make good a speed of only 4–5 knots against the wind!

Using or avoiding these currents is mainly a question of common sense since they are consistent in direction, although they can sometimes vary in speed. A glance at a current chart should indicate the best track to follow, while a distinct change in water temperature will indicate when the boat is entering or leaving a current.

PREVAILING WINDS

Much the same applies to the permanent winds that flow around the globe; some can be beneficial, some not, and often a considerable detour from the straight track is the quickest route to follow.

In the days of the old windjammers (sailing ships), vessels sailing from Australia to Europe would sooner take the hazardous easterly route round the dreaded Cape Horn rather than battle against the massive westerlies that blow constantly around the entire globe in the southern latitudes.

Examination of global wind patterns will indicate which direction is the best to take, for most winds blow constantly year round, with some minor variations. The only regions where winds are not predictable are the tropics with their windless doldrums.

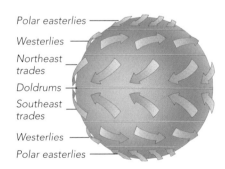

Polar easterlies
Westerlies
Northeast trades
Doldrums
Southeast trades
Westerlies
Polar easterlies

Great circle sailing

If a line were drawn between two points on the earth's surface, and then the surface was flattened out to make a chart, the straight line would become a curve, because its was originally drawn on a curved surface. Therefore, on the surface of the globe, a great circle follows the curvature of the earth, with its plane passing through the earth's centre, and it is the shortest distance between two points on the earth's surface.

Although the Mercator chart is reasonably accurate for short stretches of open sea, it is not suitable for plotting a track across an entire ocean, particularly if the track crosses higher latitudes, or is predominantly east-west. In these circumstances, a technique known as great circle sailing is used.

Meridians of longitude, and the equator, are great circles. When sailing along these, no special technique is required and a Mercator chart can be used. For other long distance tracks, a gnomonic chart (see p131) is used, as it is designed to compensate for the curvature of the earth's surface. Any course laid on it follows a great circle track – a straight line and the shortest distance across earth's surface.

There is a navigation technique for transferring a great circle track from a gnomonic to a Mercator chart, and it is well worth learning it if you plan to sail in the higher latitudes for any length of time.

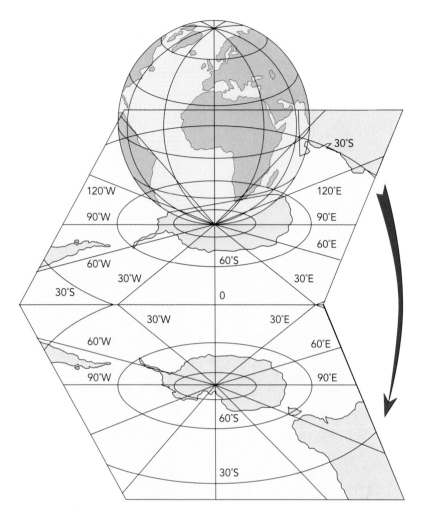

Meridians of longitude are great circles and thus appear on a chart as straight lines, as does the equator. All other straight lines on a chart, including parallels of latitude, follow a curved path across the earth's surface. The curve is toward the poles.

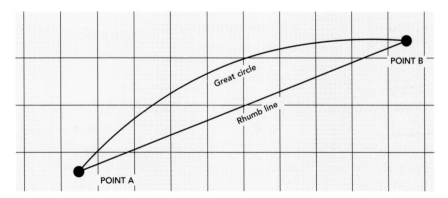

On a Mercator chart, the shortest distance between two points is shown as a curve. Despite the fact that the rhumb, or straight, line appears to be much the same length, over a long ocean passage, the curved route will always be shorter.

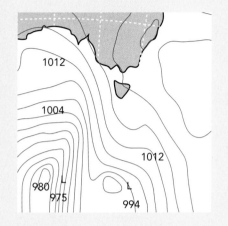  

WEATHER AND WEATHER FORECASTING

Since sailing is totally dependent on the wind, every sailor should have a working knowledge of the weather and how to predict approaching changes. Modern electronic communication makes it possible to obtain regular updates on weather patterns, but the information is mostly of a general nature, and covers large areas. A sailor needs details of weather changes which are going to affect him in the next few hours or so. Weather can change quickly, and official forecasters are not always aware of local developments, which are often created by specific conditions or topography. Knowing how the land and sea breezes work along a stretch of coastline, for example, can enable a skipper to plan his coastal passage to enjoy the most amenable sailing conditions and avoid unpleasant winds and seas.

Heavy seas are usually a good indicator that bad weather is on the way.

Apart from reading and understanding official weather maps and forecasts, it is important to be able to predict any potential change in conditions which may affect the boat in the next few hours.

Local knowledge is obviously important, but an ability to read a synoptic chart and to anticipate changes, as well as interpreting the sky signs that herald such changes, will enable the navigator to avoid the worst wind and sea conditions. A widely experienced phenomenon is the approach of a line squall at sea. Because this is a local condition, it is unlikely to be predicted by a general weather forecast other than, perhaps, as advice of an approaching front.

The only real warning a yachtsman will get is the distinctive line of black cloud approaching from some distance away, which allows the time to reduce sail ready for the savage blast of wind that heralds a squall (assuming, of course, that it arrives in daylight; if a squall comes up during the night, there may be no warning at all!)

While national forecasters may not mention squalls, everyday sailing can be influenced by a variety of local phenomena, such as the infamous southerly buster of the SE Australian coast that can scream out of a clear sky in minutes, turning a modest 15 knot (33km/hr) sea breeze into a raging storm, and catching inexperienced sailors unaware with wind speeds of up to 50 knots (92km/hr) or more.

The weather map

The basis of weather forecasting at sea is the synoptic weather map or chart. This is produced by official weather bureaux in all countries and is published in newspapers, screened on television, and transmitted by radio or weather fax, so it is readily available to everyone: farmers, fliers and boats at sea.

The map gives an overall picture of the situation across a wide area and indicates the conditions that exist at surface level, including air pressure and temperature, wind direction, warm and cold fronts and any other weather conditions which may exist at that time.

Since weather systems move fairly consistently, it is relatively easy to anticipate what systems are moving in, and what weather will be experienced over the next day or two. From that basic information, additional visual signs can provide the fine tuning for a fairly accurate local forecast.

PRESSURE SYSTEMS

High- and low-pressure systems sweep constantly across the face of the earth, generally from west to east. Forming the basis of most weather conditions, the pressure systems are shown on the synoptic chart as a series of contours, in much the same way as the contours on a map indicate the peaks and valleys of the land. These contours, called isobars, are created by lines of equal pressure. Just as,

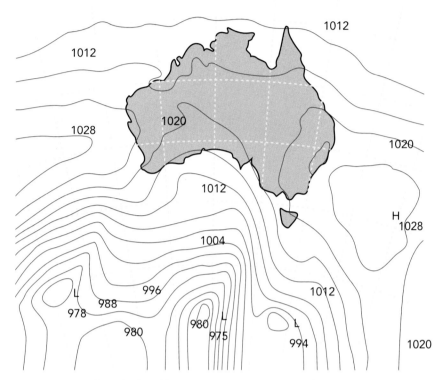

A synoptic map shows high and low pressure systems over a wide area.

on maps, the contours of hills indicate the steepness of the gradient by the spacing of the lines, so the gradients of air pressure (measured in millibars) are indicated by the spacing of the isobars.

A steep gradient creates strong winds and vice versa, so the closer the isobars, the stronger the winds. The strength of the wind is the first and, from a sailor's point of view, perhaps the most important, feature of the weather map.

Winds rotate clockwise around low-pressure systems in the southern hemisphere and anti-clockwise in the northern hemisphere. They generally follow the isobars in

terms of direction but are angled slightly in towards the centre. The opposite applies to high-pressure systems; where the winds rotate anti-clockwise around the centre of the pressure system in the southern hemisphere and clockwise in the northern hemisphere and are angled slightly outward from the line of the isobars. This provides the sailor with another important factor in his forecasting – the direction of the winds.

High- and low-pressure systems roughly alternate one after the other, which is why bad weather conditions are mostly followed by a spell of fine weather.

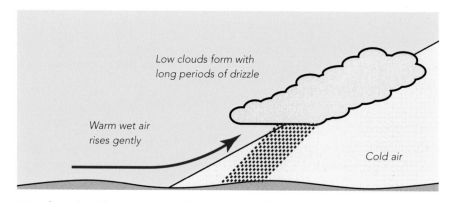

Warm fronts herald overcast skies with the prospect of light rain.

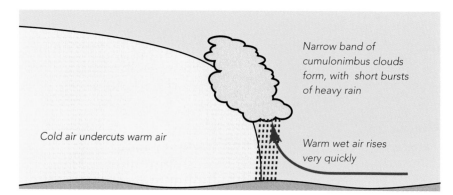

Cold fronts bring storms and heavy rain, and are best avoided by inexperienced sailors.

Low-pressure systems are the bad weather systems as they usually bring cloud, rain and strong winds. By contrast, balmy summer days will mostly be indicated by a large high-pressure area, with well spaced isobars, the sign of a fine weather system.

Strong, violent winds, like hurricanes, appear on a weather chart as a very intense low, sometimes with the appearance of a whirlpool. Wind arrows, if they are included, provide more precise information on the direction and strength of the winds; the direction indicated by the shaft of the arrow and the strength by the feathers.

FRONTS

Fronts occur when hot and cold air mix and create turbulent conditions. They indicate a change in the weather, an important factor for boats at sea. Warm fronts are milder than cold fronts, moving more slowly and usually bringing overcast skies, winds, light rain and poor visibility.

Cold fronts, on the other hand, can be very violent. They move quickly and bring strong winds and heavy rain, often with thunder, lightning and hail. They vary according to local conditions, but are usually most severe when following hot, sultry conditions. The

southerly buster is typical of a violent cold front, moving rapidly and often destructively along the coastline (see p143).

Fortunately, most cold fronts announce their arrival some hours in advance with high cirrostratus clouds. Later, huge cumulonimbus thunderclouds move in, accompanied by rain and lightning. When a cold front is close, the wind may fade to the proverbial 'calm before the storm'. This is the time to reef or drop the sails, because when the front hits, chances are the wind will scream in at full gale force.

Warm fronts, which are common in the northern hemisphere, tend to build steadily, without a period of calm beforehand.

Severe fronts usually pass quickly, but frequently leave a legacy of torn sails, capsized dinghies and grounded boats in their wake.

Cold fronts are indicated on the weather chart as a series of black triangles along a line, usually radiating from the centre of a low-pressure system; warm fronts have black half-circles.

Since weather systems move in a general west-to-east direction, the approach of a front can be anticipated. The severity of a cold front is not so easy to determine, although the closeness of the isobars, and any drastic change of wind direction behind the front, can be a guide. The best indication is the visual appearance of the sky as the storm approaches.

The trade winds

Always popular with ocean sailors because of their consistency and moderate conditions, the trade winds are so named because they were widely used by the old square-rigged trading ships making long passages in tropical and sub tropical waters.

Trade winds work on the same basic principle as the land and sea breezes but on a much large scale.

The hot tropical climate in the vicinity of the equator draws in wind from the cooler latitudes to the north and south. If the world were stationary, the winds would blow directly north and south but, because the earth is turning, they are deflected in NE and SE directions (northeast in the northern hemisphere and southeast in the southern hemisphere).

Their reliable direction and useful speed (15–30 knots/28–55 km/hr) enable yachts planning an ocean crossing to embrace good sailing conditions by running before the wind for hundreds of nautical miles with little need to adjust sails or rudder.

A favourite rig with yachts sailing before the trade winds is the twin staysail rig, in which two headsails are set out on poles, one on each side of the boat with the mainsail dropped. This rig balances the boat well and reduces the need for attention to the sails or rudder. With automatic steering, the boat will often require no attention at all,

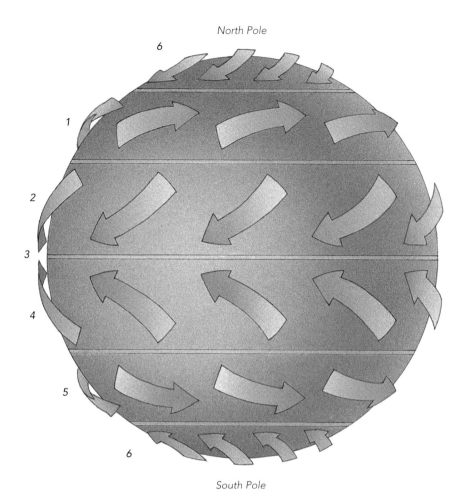

North Pole

South Pole

The major wind systems move from areas of high pressure, found at the poles and in the subequatorial regions, towards areas of low pressure, found at the equator and tropics.
1) Westerlies   2) Northeast trades   3) Equatorial trough (doldrums)
4) Southeast trades   5) Westerlies (roaring forties)
6) Polar easterlies (both North and South poles).

as long as the winds do not change. Trade winds are useful for all forms of sailing as they are not confined to specific areas of the world; other than the tropical regions, they blow across most of the oceans as well along coastlines.

Where the trade winds meet, in the equatorial regions, is the horror zone of ocean sailing known as the doldrums. Here, the trade winds drop away to be replaced by dead calms which, in the intense heat and humidity of the tropics, make life very unpleasant indeed.

In the past, lacking a motor to provide some sort of assistance, sailing ships sometimes lowered a rowing boat and put the crew to work towing the ship out of this desolate area. Nowadays sailors in the same situation simply switch on the handy 'diesel topsail'.

The quality of the scanner determines the quality of the radar image. This is an example of a long-range Open Array radar scanner.

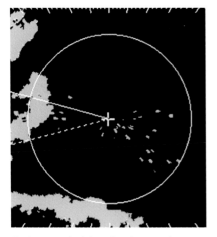

Radar is invaluable in fog, but in a busy seaway, it can be hard to interpret.

When sailing close to land in fog, every available crew member needs to be on deck.

Sailing in fog

Fog can create a nightmare situation for sailors, especially in areas where there is considerable sea traffic. Although radar has greatly reduced the risk of collision in fog, yachts sometimes do not show up on radar screens due to their low profile and the fact that they can be among large waves where they are hidden from the radar pulse.

International safety regulations require yachts sailing in fog-prone waters to carry a radar reflector on the mast. This reflects a powerful signal to the radar screen of an approaching vessel, making the yacht more visible. However, large commercial ships are notorious for their casual attitude to small craft and collisions are frequent. In most cases, either the watch keeper on the ship failed to keep a close watch on the radar screen, or a proper visual lookout was not kept.

Instruments are available which can warn of the close approach of a large ship, but in thick fog, taking avoiding action is nerve wracking when you cannot see your adversary. Most large yachts carry their own radar to avoid such situations, although this is an expensive piece of equipment and rather cumbersome for smaller boats, so it is not fitted to all craft.

Regardless of whether or not radar is carried, the Colregs (p78) require all vessels to make sound signals when navigating in fog. Most yachts carry a hand-held hooter or horn for this purpose.

RACING

Almost everyone who has an interest in sailing gets involved with racing at some stage. Whether it is as skipper, crew or even spare hand, there is something about the exhilaration and excitement of sailboat racing that gets the adrenaline working in even the least adventurous sailors. But racing is very demanding, whatever role you play in it. As the owner of the boat you can expect to be forever dipping your hand in your pocket, because racing a sailboat, particularly a keelboat, is a very expensive business. As one of the crew, racing will take up a lot of your time for, like any team sport, serious sailboat racing requires dedication, not just while racing, but also in terms of training, and preparation of the boat.

Racing in dinghies can be exhilarating, particularly at Olympic and world championship levels, where there are classes for single- and double-handed boats.

The Olympic classes

Participating in an Olympic Games is the ultimate goal for racing sailors. The events are limited to certain classes, which change from one Games to another as new and more sophisticated craft are developed. The classes for Athens 2004 comprised single-handed dinghies (Finn for men, Europe for women, and an open Laser class), double-handed dinghies (470 for both men and women, plus an open 49er class), keelboats (Star for men, Yngling for women) and the open Tornado multihull class, as well as sailboard classes for both men and women.

The 6.9m Star, designed in 1911, was the first Olympic one-design. It has raced in every Olympics, bar one, since 1932. Many of the world's top sailors learnt their skills competing in the Star class.

Getting into racing

Racing is conducted by sailing clubs under the auspices of state or national bodies and, in some cases, international organizations. So step one in getting into racing, either with your own boat or as crew for someone else's boat, is to join a suitable sailing club. Most clubs race specific types of boats, such as centreboard dinghies, multihulls or keel yachts, although some cover a number of different types and classes.

Club membership can be expensive for a boat owner, but is often less expensive if you plan to race as crew (clubs may also accept non-members as crew). However, everyone wishing to join a racing crew should obtain the required qualifications from an officially recognized sailing school or similar organization. Some sailing clubs run their own training programmes, and there are plenty of commercially run sailing schools which are accredited by official national yachting bodies to train and qualify both masters and crew for different types of racing.

As a crew member there will be considerable demand on your time at weekends, and sometimes even weekdays with long offshore races. Depending on the length of the season, this can make inroads into family time because, unlike social sailing, racing occurs on a regular basis, mostly at weekends. Each member of the crew, being

the boats can jockey for position, giving disadvantaged boats a chance to get around the mark without infringing upon the rules or causing a collision.

Details of the racing rules are published by local yacht clubs or sailing organizations, and are based on those drawn up by the International Sailing Federation (ISAF), the ultimate authority for the sport. Copies are usually available from the host club and must be studied carefully by the skipper, so that he is fully conversant with them before entering a race. Most yacht clubs use some form of performance handicap or rating system so that boats of a similar size and class compete against each other; while staggered starts allow the bigger, faster yachts to get away ahead of the smaller ones.

Successful racing requires crew members who are able to dedicate time to practising all year round in preparation for the summer racing season.

The racing rules

Racing rules, while incorporating the normal collision regulations that apply to all boats (see p78), differ in some areas because of the specific circumstances which can arise in the course of a race. For example, at a large yacht club, up to 20 or 30 boats could converge on a rounding mark, all with the aim of passing it as quickly as possible and setting off on the next leg. If the international collision rules were followed, which state that on the same tack the windward boat gives way to the leeward boat, only the leeward boat would get through, all the others, being windward boats, would have to give way. The racing rules provide a fairer system in which, prior to reaching the mark,

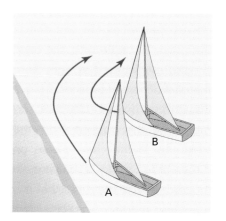

Hailing room for obstruction (calling for water). When two close hauled boats are approaching an obstruction on the same tack, the boat that is leeward (A) or ahead may hail the other boat (B) for room to allow it to tack first.

Sailing the course

The layout of courses for yacht and dinghy racing vary considerably according to the type of boats involved and the nature of the waterway in which the races are sailed. In an open bay, for example, small centreboard dinghies will most likely sail around a basic triangular course which incorporates every point of sailing. If the waterway is large and deep enough, this system may also be used for smaller keel yachts such as the Etchells or Dragons. Since these boats are not suitable for racing in rough seas (most have no self-draining cockpit) they usually keep to sheltered waters, but their course will be longer than that for sailing dinghies, and the track may vary from the basic triangular course, depending on the topography of the waterway. However, whatever the situation, the courses are usually laid to ensure that, between the start and the finish lines, the boats are tested on all points of sailing.

Offshore racing takes place around a triangular course with marker buoys laid in the open water. Longer races usually follow the coastline, using features such as islands or lighthouses as the rounding marks. Although boat performance is a factor in these races (as in any form of racing), weather, offshore currents and tidal flows play a major part in long coastal or ocean races.

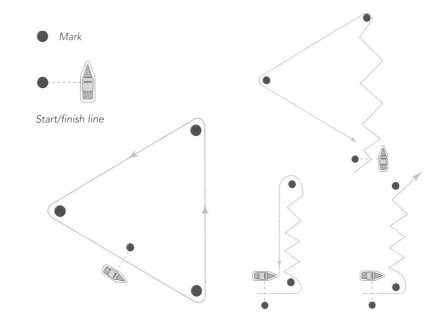

The most basic course is a simple triangle (left), which tests boats on all points of sailing, while more complex courses require boats to tack repeatedly on one or more legs.

THE START

Where possible, the start line is laid across the wind so that the first leg is a beat or tack to windward. This is aimed at giving expert skippers, and boats that have been tuned to a high degree of performance, a chance to get the jump on slower boats. Tactics play an important part on this leg of the race, perhaps more so than on any other leg. For example, since starboard tack has right of way over port tack, a boat which crosses the line on a starboard tack will gain an immediate advantage by forcing the port tack boats to give way. Because of this, all skippers will try and start on a starboard tack, creating a hectic battle for position even before the gun goes off.

Reckless *drops her spinnaker while rounding the leeward mark. Care must be taken to ensure it doesn't come down into the water.*

THE WEATHER MARK

The windward, or weather, mark is usually a buoy located directly upwind of the start line. After the tacking battle along the first leg from the start line, it is time to ease sheets and set up for a more comfortable leg, which will probably be a reaching leg.

Tuning the rig and setting the sails correctly are the important factors on this leg, and it may be possible to fly a shy spinnaker, depending on the cut of the sail and just how close to a reach the boat is sailing. Since this leg is sailed along a straight line, speed is of the essence; the helm must be used as little as possible or it will act like a brake and slow the boat down, while the sails must be set to give maximum drive.

THE LEEWARD MARK

The leeward mark calls for smart sail handling because rounding it will probably involve gybing. Before reaching the mark the boats will be jockeying for position to try and gain an advantage at the turn. If spinnakers are carried, they will need to be gybed on the mark, for there will be no time to bring them down and hoist them again when the gybe is completed. It is here that the race can get very hectic, for gybing a spinnaker, especially in strong winds, is a tricky operation, and a bad gybe or fouled spinnaker can create havoc in a group of fast-moving boats, all within centimetres of each other and all trying to round the mark at the same time!

The final leg is usually a run or broad reach, so the spinnaker may be carried to the finish line.

Racing tactics

Racing demands a high degree of sailing and boat-handling skills on the part of the skipper and crew, but clever use of racing tactics can often gain an added advantage that will give the boat an edge on the rest of the fleet. Sailboat races of any kind involve tactics, and a skipper who knows his boat and is skilled in race tactics will always be at the head of the fleet.

Some tactics are simple, like sailing up behind an opponent on a spinnaker run in order to blanket him and cause his spinnaker to collapse, or using the rules to gain advantage on the turn around a mark. Others are more involved.

In long ocean races, where navigation can be a key factor, such as the Newport to Bermuda race, for instance, the main leg sometimes ends at a buoy well out of sight of land. Locating a small buoy in an open expanse of sea after a long haul without landmarks can test the skills of even the best navigators, who may find themselves in the unenviable position of being able to win or lose the race purely on the accuracy of their navigation.

Long distance offshore racing, such as the Sydney to Hobart open water race, requires a different set of tactics from those employed in close racing around the buoys in harbours and estuaries, where there can often be 'traffic jams' at the turning marks. Out at sea, there is no room for error.

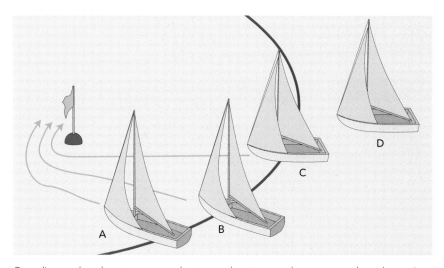

Rounding marks: when two or more boats are about to round or pass a mark or obstruction on the same side, an outside boat must give way to any boat overlapping it on the inside. Therefore, A gives way to B and C, but B gives way only to C. Boats clear astern may only establish an inside overlap when the boat ahead is more than two boat lengths from the mark or obstruction, so D may not ask A, B or C for room (call for water).

These boats are racing on a broad reach in light winds, with each one trying to cover the boat in front in an effort to collapse its spinnaker and slow it down.

CRUISING

Where once 'cruising' in sailing terms meant either overnight sailing in local waters or spending a lot of time sailing your boat to distant cruising waters, the definition has expanded in recent decades. Nowadays, people fly direct to their chosen waterway and charter a boat for their cruising holiday. Indeed, chartering has become a favourite way of spending a holiday afloat, with the cost of flying and charter fees offset by the savings in time and money maintaining your own boat, as well as transporting it to the cruising grounds. While many 'home' waters provide excellent scope for waterborne holidays, even in the higher latitudes, the lure of exotic tropical destinations, extensively portrayed in travel brochures, is hard to resist. When compared with exotic waterways such as the Mediterranean, the Caribbean and the Great Barrier Reef, most of the northern and southern cruising grounds struggle to meet the challenge.

Charter companies offer the latest in comfortable, spacious and well-maintained boats that are able to meet the requirements of families or groups of friends who want an enjoyable holiday at sea. However, you must meet certain sailing standards before you can hire a boat.

Chartering

One of the greatest advantages of chartering is that, in tropical or subtropical locations, cruising is not just limited to the summer, it can be enjoyed for most of the year. Within a few hours of leaving an ice-bound London or New York you can step aboard a comfortable, fully equipped yacht and be ready to sail out onto warm, crystal clear waters and anchor in picturesque tropical bays.

Of course, compared with sailing your own boat, you are limited in where you can go and what you can do but, since most charter companies operate in exciting and unusual locations, that is rarely a major problem for an adventurous sailor looking for a fun holiday.

You don't even have to worry about sailing it, as charter boats can be hired complete with a professional skipper and crew.

Another advantage of chartering is that all the mundane chores of owning a boat are taken care of. Maintenance, the bugbear of boat ownership, is handled by the char-

ter company, as are insurance and damage repair in the event of a mishap. As a general rule, charter boats come equipped with all sailing and safety gear, plus modern navigation equipment, so there is virtually nothing to think about other than what clothes to pack and, on a yacht in a tropical location, that's rarely a problem.

Whether or not the costs of chartering versus owning work out equitably depends on many factors, but in terms of convenience, chartering wins hands down.

Before taking the plunge, however, you need to satisfy yourself that the boat and the conditions of charter match what you have in mind for your sailing holiday, but otherwise, there is literally nothing to do but get yourself to the departure port.

If you are not qualified to handle larger yachts, enquiries about paid crew must be made, although this will increase the overall cost.

Yachting magazines list many international charter companies and their preferred locations and indicate whether they offer bareboat (sail-it-yourself) or crewed vessels. A phone call or email can resolve most immediate queries, then there is only the plane booking to be made and your sailing holiday is assured.

Owning a cruising boat

If sailing someone else's boat is not your thing, or you have no intention of sailing far from home, or even if you enjoy just 'messing about in boats' at weekends and holidays, then owning your own cruising boat is a better option. There is a great deal of enjoyment to be had primping and polishing and just generally keeping the boat in shape. Quite a few yachties enjoy maintaining their boats, and it certainly engenders a lot of pride when you take a sparkling, impeccably kept boat out of the marina to the obvious admiration of the crowd on the quayside.

Chartering offers the pleasures of cruising but none of the day-to-day problems of boat-owning. It also means being able to holiday in a different place every year.

There are many avenues of pleasure to be had from owning your own cruising yacht and sailing it in waters close to home. Taking family and friends out for day or weekend trips, learning how to handle the boat under different conditions and qualifying for official certificates in navigation and boat handling all add to the enjoyment of owning the boat, and are a reward in their own right to many skippers. Not for them the rather clinical and unemotional act of hiring and sailing a strange boat; they prefer the hustle and bustle of working in dirty jeans, the delight in planning their own passage and the exhilaration of handling the helm of their own pride and joy as it heads out to sea.

If there is such a thing as the ideal cruising boat, it would be one that is of good size (so that family and friends can be accommodated comfortably on board), that has all the requirements for safe navigation, and is relatively easy to handle. Most cruising families do not enjoy

Galley storage is often limited.

Freshly baked bread is always a treat!

A large luxury catamaran offers a range of comforts that are seldom found on small boats.

thrashing through gale force winds and big seas, hanging on for dear life with their hands, teeth and anything else that is of use. They prefer a yacht which, if it is caught in a blow, can be quickly and comfortably snugged down with the minimum of crew on deck or, better still, has a big diesel motor under the cockpit which will take it swiftly into a calm, sheltered harbour.

Keep these things in mind when considering purchasing a cruising boat. A fast racing boat, however sporty and sleek it may be, is likely to be wet and uncomfortable with only pipe berths and a tiny gas stove to brew up tins of soup or pots of coffee for the crew.

To make things as homely as possible, most sailing families like comfortable bunks, a good-sized galley with a fridge, a decent toilet and hot-water shower and, in cold climates, good heating. Full headroom in the cabin can also make a huge difference, especially to tall people, as constantly bending over takes much of the fun out of living aboard. Good ventilation is essential if a number of people are to be sleeping on board, especially if all the hatches are closed because of bad weather. Small points, but they will do much to win over a family that has misgivings about acquiring a cruising yacht.

As one long-time sailor quipped: 'I've swopped warm beer and cold water for cold beer and hot showers, and my family and crew have never been happier!'

Maintenance

The amount of work involved in owning a yacht varies according to the type of boat, its construction and how frequently it is used.

A fibreglass boat is relatively easy to maintain in the water; just an occasional polish of the hull and a run round the working parts with the grease gun should be all that is needed. The sails may need an occasional trip to the sail maker to repair chafed or worn stitching, but that is no chore, especially as there is usually a sail maker based somewhere near the marina or dock. The once-a-year hauling out for anti-fouling and to check the underwater fittings is the only work of any consequence required, and even that usually takes only one or two days on the slipway.

If the hull is timber then the work can become more demanding. Sunlight plays havoc with painted or varnished timber, so the cabin and deck need to be maintained throughout the year. If the hull is painted it will require a touch-up of damaged areas every now and then or, at worst, a complete hull repaint if the wear and tear is severe. Slipping at least once a year is a vitally important chore.

Apart from applying a new coat of anti-fouling, the timber of the hull must be carefully examined for any infestation of worm or marine borer. Some timber boats in tropical waters need hauling out more than once a year.

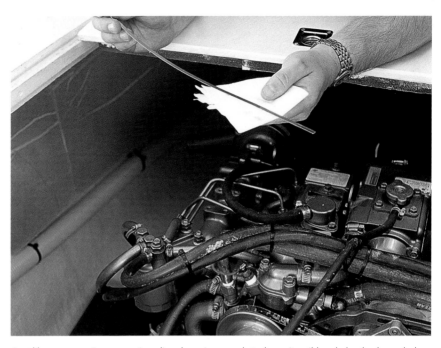

Just like a car engine, a marine diesel engine needs to have its oil level checked regularly.

Preparing for a cruise

If you are chartering, there is little to do but show up at the marina or dock on the designated day and go through the paperwork with the charter company. However, owning a boat requires a lot of preparation, particularly if you are planning an extended cruise.

Firstly, you have to ensure that the boat is fully equipped in terms of sailing and navigational gear, safety equipment and food. Some cruising areas, especially islands, are fairly remote, and having equipment problems or running out of food or fresh water can mean interrupting a pleasant holiday in a secluded anchorage to trek to a port some way away.

In planning a long passage on a boat, it is important to have a thorough check list and run through it before leaving your home port if problems later are to be avoided.

A minimum check would include all electronic gear to ensure that it is running correctly, and to calibrate items such as radio and GPS, which is best done by taking the boat into clear water, away from headlands and buildings which can interfere with the signals. Many ports have a GPS checkpoint marked on the chart somewhere near the entrance.

The compass error should be checked by swinging it (see p119), and the sextant needs to be given its routine mirror check (see p133). The log can be checked against a measured distance in the harbour and the sounder checked against the chart as well as with a lead line.

The motor must be inspected as it is likely to be well-used when

Water tanks are usually filled from an inlet opening in the deck.

When provisioning for a long distance cruise, always add 25 per cent more than you think you need. Fresh fruit and vegetables don't last long, so stock up whenever you are in port.

cruising, for moving around bays or estuaries as well as getting to a destination when the wind dies.

It is wise to carry a range of tools and spare parts, especially for the engine, as assistance can be hard to find when you are many nautical miles from civilization.

FOOD AND WATER

Food and water need to be calculated according to the number of people on board, the isolation of the cruising venue, and the keeping qualities of the stores.

Refrigeration is always limited on a boat and, while vegetables such as onions and potatoes will keep fresh for some time, fruit usually goes off fairly quickly.

If there is no likelihood of replenishing perishables for some time, tinned products may be the only practical solution. Tins can be stowed under the cabin floors and in the bilges where they are nicely out of the way until required. It is important to remove all paper labels and write the contents on the can with a waterproof pen

before stowing them because if water gets into the bilges the pumps will quickly be choked with soggy paper. Dried, dehydrated or long-life foods are also suitable for lengthy storage.

Be wary of water taken aboard at smaller ports, especially in the tropics. Fresh water from an uncertain source can easily contain unwanted bugs, so it may be necessary to purify it, or carry bottled water for drinking, using the water in the tanks solely for washing up and showering.

It is regarded as good seamanship to fly your national flag from the stern when entering a foreign port. In addition, a courtesy flag of the country you are visiting should be flown from the mast or cross-trees (spreaders).

Encounters with officialdom

If your cruise is confined mostly to home waters, even some distance from your home port, there should be no problems with immigration, customs and other authorities.

Some ports require a visitor's fee, especially if it is necessary to berth alongside a wharf or marina, but other than routine checks of the boat's papers and perhaps an inspection to see that you haven't picked up any contraband or illegal immigrants on your way around the coast, the authorities should have little interest in a boat that has not strayed out of its home waters. However, it is important to contact the port authorities before arriving at your destination and not arouse suspicions by sneaking in unobserved. Much depends on each individual port, but to avoid having problems with any authorities, a radio call to the harbour master or coastguard beforehand should help to dispel any doubts they may have about your intentions.

Entering foreign ports, of course, is a different ball game. Here the whole gamut of officialdom must be confronted, depending on which port, which nationality, and how tough they are on visiting vessels. Once again, the secret is to be totally open. Report in by radio well before arrival and ask what they need so that when you enter port you can have the paperwork ready.

Make sure you fly the national flag of the country you are visiting (called a courtesy flag) from the mast or spreaders and your own national flag at the stern. Some countries get touchy about these things and it is best to smooth the path right at the outset.

Three favourite cruising venues

While not everyone agrees on what makes an ideal cruising waterway, it cannot be denied that there are certain factors that contribute, notably a year-round warm climate, crystal clear water, lots of good, safe anchorages, and interesting ports or islands.

That mostly means tropical or sub-tropical latitudes, certainly as far as the climate is concerned. Of course, there are some really interesting cruising waters in colder climes – the Norwegian or Swedish fjords, or the Maine coastline, for example, but these are mostly not viable for a large part of the year and can be somewhat restricted even during the summer season in terms of swimming and similar outdoor activities. While temperate islands are very picturesque and interesting, they do not have quite the appeal that the waving palms and horseshoe beaches of exotic tropical cruising waters offer for family holidays.

The following pages offer a very brief description of some of the more popular cruising waters around the world. They are not intended to be exhaustive, merely to serve as a hint of what you can expect when you cruise in these regions. Of course, it goes without saying that, when planning a cruising trip, you should obtain as much up-to-date information as possible on your destination.

Paradise found? The ability to sail away to discover unknown lands (and seas) is part of the attraction of owning, or chartering, a cruising yacht.

THE CARIBBEAN

The crystal blue waters of the Caribbean Sea are surrounded by perfect cruising venues.

The Lesser Antilles island chain, which curves around the eastern perimeter, from Trinidad, off the coast of Brazil, to Puerto Rico, is cruising paradise. Picturesque tropical islands, large and small, with equally picturesque ports and towns, stud this part of the Caribbean like a gemstone necklace, providing every kind of idyllic holiday a family could wish for. (Indeed, the islands of St Vincent and the Grenadines are nicknamed the 'Gems of the Antilles'.)

Navigation is normally quite easy, although the hurricane season, between July and November, requires a careful watch, as yachts caught in the open sea would have little chance of survival.

At the first sign of a hurricane heading towards your area, boats should make for the nearest port where, although still vulnerable, at least the crew can get ashore to safety if the need arises (see p150).

History is alive and well in the Caribbean and remnants of the colonial past provide intrigue and interest to the tropical lushness of many of the islands. French and British names, relics of their colonial origins, are often incongruous: Portsmouth and Plymouth lie on either side of Basse-Terre, while Georgetown and Soufriere are on adjoining islands.

A traditional schooner revels in the trade wind conditions off Antigua. The annual sailing week held here attracts boats and sailors from all over the world.

The perfect climate makes sailing easy, and the clear water is ideal for scuba diving in the many little bays and inlets of the islands.

The Caribbean is one of the most visited waterways in the world. The upside of the region's popularity is that facilities in the ports are good and well-structured to cater for cruising yachts, and food and clean water are readily available everywhere. Despite the crowds though, there is always some quiet, isolated bay where you can leave the world behind.

Although there are literally thousands of miles of cruising waters around the coasts of the islands, as well as along the mainland that fringes the Caribbean, the most popular region for cruising is the eastern chain of small islands in the Windward, Leeward and Virgin island groups.

The Virgin Islands are called the 'capital of the cruising world', while one of the main centres, Antigua, is renowned for its annual sailing week, as well as the magnificent sailing vessels that berth in

Marigot Bay on St Lucia, in the Windward Islands, is typical of the sheltered bays that attract yachts to the Lesser Antilles. Sailing in the Caribbean is usually easy, with comfortable downwind passages between many of the island groups.

Nelson's Dockyard or anchor in the pretty town of English Harbour.

From the Lesser Antilles and Virgin islands, the Caribbean island chain moves westward towards larger islands such as Puerto Rico, the Dominican Republic, Haiti, Jamaica and Cuba, then on to the Gulf of Mexico at the western end. Here the Spanish influence takes over, as seen in the names and culture of the islands.

Further out in the Atlantic lie the Bahamas, an extensive archipelago of delightful islands ideal for cruising holidays. They are within easy reach of Fort Lauderdale, on the US mainland, where many of the big charter companies that serve the Caribbean are based.

All forms of chartering are available in this tropical paradise, from family bareboat to the latest luxury catamarans – the choice being determined only by your sailing preference and price range.

Access to all the main islands is easy by air, so the only effort required is transferring your luggage (in soft, easily stowable bags, of course!) from the airport to the boat of your choice, and possibly a quick trip to the local shops for provisions. (On request, most charter companies will equip the boat with basic groceries, so all you have to do is stock up with fresh foods for the next day or two.)

Once you have completed any formalities and gone through the hand-over procedures, you can set sail and be under way, heading for your first night at sea.

SOUTH PACIFIC

The legendary islands of the South Pacific cover a vast area of ocean. Many are scattered so far apart that the most inhibiting factor in cruising here is having to cross large stretches of open water, firstly to get to the region and then to get from one island to another.

The South Pacific contrasts markedly with the Caribbean and Mediterranean in that centres of civilization are few and far between. While the islands themselves are among the most beautiful in the world, they are often isolated and lacking in facilities.

Extended cruising in the South Pacific is really for the sailor who has a great deal of time to spare and wants to get away from it all; families with limited holiday time need to select one island group. Fiji is a good example, where there are relatively short hops between the main and offshore islands as opposed to the vast distances between the more widely spread island groups such as Melanesia, Micronesia, Hawaii and Tahiti.

Fiji, the Solomons, Vanuatu and New Caledonia all have delightful cruising waterways with numerous islands and cays that make for ideal holidays. They are well set-up to cater for cruising boats, although there is the problem of getting to them via long stretches of open ocean.

Fiji is over 1700 nautical miles from Australia across open seas

A secluded anchorage on Hamilton Island, in the Whitsundays, part of the Great Barrier Reef. While scuba diving is the main attraction here, cruising is also popular.

with only a few small islands en route, although the delights of the Fijian group provide a fine reward for the effort of crossing from Australia or New Zealand.

A more popular cruising waterway, which does not involve long ocean passages, is Australia's Great Barrier Reef, where the islands are contained in one fairly closely linked chain within easy reach of the mainland. Major cities on the coast offer excellent facilities along most of the 2000km (1200 miles) of the reef, while uninhabited sandy cays and islets offer get-away-from-it-all locations, each

with its own anchorage inside an isolated coral atoll. By contrast, resort islands, such as Hamilton and Hayman, offer five-star luxury and facilities akin to those of the Caribbean, while still providing all the natural wonders that have established the Great Barrier Reef as a world heritage site.

The waters inside the reef, which acts as a breakwater to the ocean swells of the Pacific, provide good sailing. Crystal clear water, beneath which can be seen colourful corals and a profusion of fish of all kinds, makes for a perfect family holiday, while the tropical climate keeps

Small islets dot the lagoons around Fiji, where the crystal clear water and vibrant coral reefs invite exploration. Despite being 'miles from anywhere', the islands of the South Pacific offer a wide variety of cultural, environmental and sailing discoveries.

both air and sea temperatures in the ideal comfort zone all year round. The tropics can become hot in mid-summer, but the cooling SE trades act as an efficient air conditioner, keeping temperatures to a perfect cruising level.

Navigation can be tricky if you wander off the shipping routes. The whole region has a mass of outlying reefs and shoal patches which are often unmarked and difficult to spot until it is too late. The main shipping channel, which runs through the centre of the reef, past myriad islands and cays, is charted and well-marked, but outside that,

care is necessary, for grounding on coral can play havoc with the hull of a boat, and cause damage to the delicate reef.

Being in the trade wind belt, the prevailing wind is the SE trade which provides excellent sailing conditions, although the northern regions can experience cyclones between November and March. A cyclone watch is maintained along the coast and cyclone warnings are broadcast when one is moving into the area. Tidal ranges are very high, in some places up to 9m (30ft), and must be taken into consideration when navigating.

Across the Tasman Sea, New Zealand has some magnificent waterways for cruising, with the most popular being the Bay of Islands, on the North Island, where the sailing, cruising and deep-sea fishing are legendary. From a spectacular point of view, Milford Sound is world-class, but getting there involves a lengthy hop down a fairly exposed coastline in order to enter the sound from seaward. The Marlborough Sounds, on the north of the South Island, are not as spectacular, but still offer pleasant, quiet cruising waters and delightful surroundings.

MAINTENANCE

Few sailors enjoy the chores of maintaining their boat; most would rather utilize any time spent on board in racing or cruising or just relishing the delights of being afloat. Unfortunately, the harsh environment in which boats are kept is not kind, and they tend to need constant maintenance if they are to remain in good shape. Sun, wind and weather play havoc with painted surfaces, and will even take the shine off normally maintenance-free fibreglass finishes. As any boat owner will agree, nothing looks worse than a poorly maintained boat, whether it be an ocean going yacht or a centreboard dinghy. Some boats require more maintenance than others, depending mostly on the material from which they are built, their age, and how well they have been cared for.

Newly varnished timber adds greatly to the appearance of a boat but requires frequent maintenance to keep it looking good.

Caulking is forced into seams between timber planks to make them watertight.

Boats left swinging on a mooring in all weather will deteriorate faster than trailer boats taken home and kept under cover. The secret is to keep on top of maintenance all year round and not neglect it. A boat which is looked after consistently will retain its appearance far longer than one which is left to the ravages of the elements and only maintained spasmodically.

While major repair work will probably need to be handed over to a shipwright, regular maintenance to keep the boat looking good and in sound condition can mostly be handled by the crew, particularly during the winter, when there is less sailing activity.

Timber hulls

Timber boats require far more maintenance than boats made from fibreglass, although a steel yacht may need more work than either timber or fibreglass.

CLEANING

Timber boats are mostly painted or varnished. Provided the paint surface has not been scored or otherwise damaged, light marks can be cleaned from the high gloss finish with warm, soapy water or a light detergent. More severe marks need stronger detergents or polishes, but care must be taken with these as they are likely to scuff the surface of the paintwork and leave dull patches on the high

gloss, spoiling the appearance of the hull. If it is done carefully however, small areas can be touched up using a can of gloss spray paint or lacquer to restore the original appearance. For really stubborn stains, or where the paint has been damaged, light wet and dry sandpaper will be necessary, but this inevitably damages the gloss surface, requiring a touch-up with spray paint. If this does not restore the original appearance, a full repaint may be necessary.

PATCHING

If the timber beneath the paint has been damaged, it must be repaired before the surface can be repainted. Serious damage may need surgery to remove the damaged areas and replace them with new wood, which requires the expertise of a shipwright.

Gouges, cracks and lesser damage can mostly be patched using an epoxy-type filler compound. These mostly come in a two-pack form and must be used soon after being mixed. The filler is forced into cracks and holes with a flat putty knife and then smoothed off flush with the surface. After the filler has cured it can be sanded back flush with the surrounding surface and built up with coats of paint to restore the surface to its original condition.

PAINTING

The secret to any good paint job lies in the preparation of the surface to be painted. This applies equally to the first paint job and to the repainting of previously painted surfaces. Timber that has not been painted before must have all holes, cracks and open grain filled before hard sanding and applying a coat of primer. Some paint manufacturers claim primer is not required, but the maritime environment is harsh, so it is probably advisable to use primer for new paint jobs.

Separate undercoat and finishing coats are then applied, with each coat sanded back using fine wet and dry paper. Although each new sanding tends to degrade the appearance of the previous surface, it is the most important part of

Above and right: Preparing the surface by sanding and applying a protective undercoat will help prolong the life, and enhance the finish, of a timber hull.

painting if a high-quality finish is required. Without hard sanding between coats, the final coat will not provide the mirror-like finish that makes the boat look its best.

Previously painted surfaces must first be stabilized by removing all flaking and loose paint before being sanded back with coarse paper to create a firm base for the new coat. Sanding with a finer grade paper will then create a suitable surface on which to rebuild the paint job, using wet and dry paper between each coat, as described before.

Primer may not be necessary unless the paint has been taken back to bare timber, but the subsequent build-up and sanding back between coats must be every bit as painstakingly carried out as it would be for the original coat.

There is no question that spray painting produces the finest finish, but it requires more preparation and skill than brush painting. Unless spray painting is handled by an expert, the result can be a disaster, not only to the paint surface itself, but to anything in the vicinity. Although expensive, a full hull paint job is probably best turned over to the yard for expert spray painting.

Fibreglass hulls

Some fibreglass hulls are painted, but most obtain their high gloss finish from the gel coat, which is the outermost layer of resin in the fibreglass laminate. This is sprayed onto the inside of the highly polished surface of the mould when the boat is being laid up then, when the boat is popped out of the mould, the high gloss of the mould is transferred to the exterior of the boat's hull. If a gel coat is not used, the hull must be painted by the boat builder.

CLEANING

Cleaning a gel coat surface on a fibreglass hull is not dissimilar to cleaning a painted hull. However, greater care is required to prevent damage to the high gloss surface of the gel coat, because it is very difficult to repaint an area which has lost its gloss.

Unlike a fibreglass surface that has been painted, a gel coat can rarely be re-sprayed in patches, and will almost certainly look patchy regardless of whether it has been dulled by the cleaning process or touched up with paint.

Soapy warm water or light detergent are fine as cleaners. Some of the patent fibreglass polishes will do the job well, However, take care with anything harsh, including some polishes, as it is very easy to rub off the fine gloss and leave a dull patch. To be safe, test the cleaner on a small area first.

A high pressure hose is used to clean the underwater areas of the hull.

Some fibreglass yachts have a coloured gel coat, which can fade as the sun bleaches out the colour.

Over time, water pollution or marine growth can stain the waterline areas of the hull and cause the gel coat to discolour. Polish can sometimes remove these stains but, in most cases, the only way to restore the pristine appearance is a coat of fresh paint, polyurethane being the most widely used. This will require a complete paint job, since trying to cover different areas will result in the hull having a patchy appearance.

PATCHING

The most likely cause of minor damage to a fibreglass hull skin is gouging, where the gel coat is chipped or torn, exposing the laminate beneath. If the gouge is no deeper than the gel coat, it can be patched with resin filler and then sanded off and painted. If the laminate beneath has been damaged, it may be necessary to rebuild the structure of the skin with glass fibres, in the form of chopped strand or mat, and resin. This is not a difficult process, but care is needed to ensure that the finished

A fresh coat of paint is applied to the newly cleaned keel of a boat that has been slipped for regular maintenance work.

repair work is flush with the surrounding surface. If, after sanding, it still has a pockmarked appearance area, a resin filler must be used and then sanded with wet and dry paper and spray painted to restore the gloss finish.

Cracks, chips and other minor surface damage can also be filled with resin filler and then finished in the same way.

Major damage involving structural sections may need special treatment and should be handed over to the yard. Osmosis, which occurs when water gets between the gel coat and the underlying fibreglass layer, also requires professional treatment. (See p187.)

PAINTING

Some boat owners use gel coat to restore repaired patches to their previous high gloss condition, but most favour a polyurethane paint. Gel coat is not easy for amateurs to handle, whereas polyurethane is little different to normal domestic paint and is relatively simple for the average DIYer to handle.

If a completely new paint job is required, then a planned system using one company's products, from primer through to topcoat, is best, as mixing different brands can sometimes have unexpected results. International Yacht Paints' complete system, which is used by many professional boat builders, comprises Interfill 835, Interprotect, Perfection Undercoat, Reaction Lacquer and Interspray 900.

The furling gear on a roller furling headsail.

Gooseneck fittings are subject to hard wear and tear.

Maintaining the rigging

Most standing rigging uses marine grade stainless steel wire rope which requires little in the way of maintenance. It is not vulnerable to severe rust and is very strong, but can suffer from fatigue with extensive use and, once this sets in, it deteriorates very quickly. It is important to keep an eye aloft for any rusted or broken strands, the first sign that a problem could be developing. All rigging should be checked regularly, because it takes only one shroud or stay to part, and the mast will fall, with potentially disastrous results.

A lubricant should be used to keep the turnbuckles (rigging screws) free, and locking wire secured around them to prevent them unwinding when the lee rigging is slack.

Although winter maintenance time is when the mast is taken down and a full check made of the rigging, regular checks throughout the sailing season will ensure that it is in good shape and unlikely to spring any nasty surprises during summer racing or cruising.

Wire running rigging is softer and less rigid than standing rigging and is often bent at quite acute angles over sheaves at the masthead or on deck, where wear and tear first starts to appear. Halyards take a lot of strain and should be prime target when checking the gear, especially where winches are used to tension the sails.

Synthetic ropes, which may also be used for halyards and are always used for sheets, may show signs of chafe or wear over time, but will rarely part unexpectedly. Provided they are replaced when they reach their 'use-by', or expiry, time, synthetic ropes should present few major problems in the course of normal sailing.

Weatherproof covers protect the boat and its gear from both rain and sun.

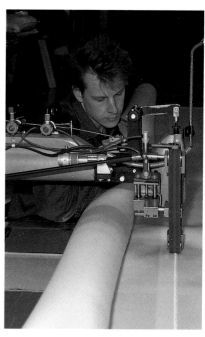

Mending sails is best left to professionals, who have the right equipment.

The sails

Sails are probably the most vulnerable of all the working gear on a sailboat. They come in for a great deal of punishment and are often in need of attention. After a hard sail it is wise to check each sail across its surface and down the edges, because the proverbial stitch in time is never truer than when applied to sails. Apart from flogging in wild weather, the chafe of rigging against a sail is likely to destroy the stitching. Unless caught in time, what begins as a small seam opening can quickly run across an entire sail panel.

The leech is a very vulnerable area, as this tends to flap when the mainsail is eased through a gust of wind or, in the case of a headsail, when it is not sheeted on correctly.

Because of the complex shape cut into a sail, any repairs must be done by a qualified sail maker; this is definitely not a job for mum's sewing machine!

Sailcloth tends to stretch with age and use, and this causes the sails to 'belly', which accentuates flapping and increases stress on the stitching. There is really no cure for this; once the sailcloth stretches there is little a sail maker can do to restore it to its original shape and a new sail is mostly necessary.

Chafed areas can be doubled up or reinforced with additional cloth (some sail makers build reinforcing into areas of the sail where chafe is likely to affect them).

Folding the sails correctly after use will not only retain their shape when next taken out of the bag,

but also reduce wear and tear on the cloth. Racing sails must always be carefully folded and stowed, never left on the boom or furled around the forestay.

The synthetic material used for sails is generally rot-free, but it can become grimy or stained, in which case the sails need to be washed gently with a warm soapy solution; not strong detergents.

Cruising mainsails left on the boom or self-furling headsails left in position on the forestay, must be covered to protect them from atmospheric damage, particularly in city harbours and estuaries where chemical and industrial pollution, as well as the ultraviolet rays of the sun, will eventually damage the material and cause the sail to deteriorate.

The underwater hull

Maintenance on the underside of a keel yacht's hull can only be done when the boat is out of the water. Centreboard dinghies and other trailer boats can be maintained in the garage when the boat is taken home, but the wetted surface of boats which are kept in the water all the time can only be examined and maintained during the annual hauling out on a slipway or hard.

In cold climates, boats may be left on the hard throughout winter, so there is plenty of time to examine the hull and fix any problems. In warmer zones, boats are hauled out, worked on, anti-fouled, and returned to the water straight away.

SLIPPING

In order to prevent marine growth attaching to the bottom of the hull and slowing the boat's movement through the water, an anti-fouling composition is painted on the wetted surface when the boat is slipped. When the hull is taken from the water and landed in a cradle, the weed, coral or slime attached to the bottom can be hosed away with pressure hoses, then finished with scrubbing brushes or scrapers, leaving the skin clean and ready for a new coat of anti-fouling composite.

Traditionally, the active ingredient was copper, which leaches out of the paint, preventing weed and shell from attaching to the hull, but this is now prohibited in many European countries. Anti-fouling is

A crane puts a keelboat back into the water after its annual maintenance haul-out.

effective for a season, but in warmer waters, when the racing season extends for much of the year, racing yachts may haul out more than once to ensure there is no growth to affect their performance. Some anti-fouling mixtures are specially designed for racing yachts, others for cruising yachts.

As soon as the underwater areas have been painted, the yacht is placed back in the water to prevent the composite from drying out and losing its effectiveness.

CAREENING

If there is no slipway or lift available, as is often the case when cruising in remote islands, then the boat will

need to be careened. This entails landing the boat on a level bottom at high tide and allowing it to rest on its side as the tide falls so that the hull can be scrubbed and cleaned before the next tide moves in. (The boat should be propped up to avoid any possibility of flooding the hull on the incoming tide.)

If there is not time to complete all the repair work and apply the new coat of anti-fouling before the next high tide, the procedure must be repeated when the tide falls again.

In some places there is plenty of time between tides, but in others, where there are severe tidal anomalies, work may have to be spread over more than one tide.

Maintenance can sometimes be a race against the tide.

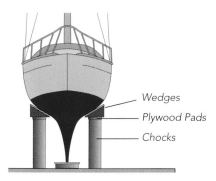

Wedges
Plywood Pads
Chocks

When careening, it is vital to place the props so the hull and keel are supported.

While on the hard for maintenance, the boat must be supported by a cradle or props.

Motor maintenance

If the motor is fitted inside the boat, maintenance can be carried out at any time as required. If it is an outboard, it can be sent ashore for maintenance by the dealer.

Routine inboard maintenance usually consists of changing the sump and gearbox oil and inspecting the fuel, oil and air filters, as well as checking the header tank levels, plugs (petrol motor) or injectors (diesel) and belts.

Major repair work is best turned over to the the mechanics in the marina workshop.

The most vulnerable part of a marine motor is the cooling system. Sea water is not usually used as a coolant in large engines as it causes internal corrosion which will soon wreck the motor, rendering it inoperable. Because of this, most marine motors have a closed circuit fresh water cooling system. This may take various forms, the most common being an enclosed system with either a header tank or heat transfer piping, depending on the manufacture and fitting of the individual motor.

Corrosion and osmosis

Boats kept on a mooring or alongside a marina are constantly in contact with salt water, giving rise to a number of maintenance problems.

The potential for marine worm to eat into the hull of a timber boat has already been described (see p25), but there are other problems which can affect all boats, even fibreglass and steel craft.

Corrosion, mostly in the form of rust, is a major problem on the hulls of steel boats and with metal fittings on other craft. With an aluminium hull, electrolytic corrosion

A sacrificial anode that has been attacked by galvanic action.

Underwater metal fittings must be protected from galvanic action.

The propeller shaft can only be maintained when it is out of the water.

can eat away the metal leaving a white powder, particularly when the aluminium is in contact with another metal.

Stainless steel and Monel (a patented, corrosion resistant alloy), are the only metals that are generally free of corrosion in a marine environment. Bronze, brass, copper and aluminum are the metals most affected by corrosion. When they make contact with another metal, such as a bronze propeller and a stainless steel shaft, or a brass fitting on an aluminium mast, corrosion will quickly eat away one

of the metals. To prevent this from occurring, insulating material is placed between the two metals or, in the case of the propeller, a sacrificial anode is used to attract the electrolytic action away from the propeller. The anode pad is gradually destroyed, but the propeller will be saved.

Osmosis is a problem that affects only fibreglass boats. It occurs when water gets under the laminate and is first noticed as bubbles or blisters in the gel coat on the underwater areas of the hull. Poor quality fibreglass, or the incorrect

laying up of the laminate when building, allows the gel coat to become permeated when it is constantly immersed in water, and a blister forms beneath the skin. Unless osmosis is treated promptly it can lead to a complete breakdown of the laminate and the subsequent delamination of the hull. If this occurs, the boat should be turned over to the marina workshop as repairs can be extensive and require expert handling.

PHOTOGRAPHIC CREDITS

Cover:		36 b	NHIL/NC	87	Ray	127	NHIL	168	CC
Front	PPL/AM	37	PEP	88	CC	128	NHIL	169 tl &r	NHIL/NC
Front tr	NHIL/NC	41	NHIL/NC	89	DG	129 t	NHIL	169 br	DG
Front br	PA	42 l	CC	90	NHIL/MN	129 b	DPPI	170	Inpra
Back t	CC	42 c	NHIL/MN	91	KS	130 l	SIL/PG	171	NC
Back c	PEP	42 r	CC	93	Kos	130 r	CC	172	TI/AH
Back b	NC	43	CC	94	TL	130 c	NHIL/PG	173	RHPL
Spine	DG	44	PG	95	CC	131	PB	174	NC
1	NHIL/NA	46	PG	96	Kos/GM-R	132	NHIL	175	PB/PB
3	OI	47	NHIL/MN	98	CC	133	NHIL	176	Kos/CB
4	CC	48	NHIL/MN	100	HH/PC	134	DPPI	177	Kos/BG
6 l	NHIL/MN	49	NHIL/MN	101	OvdW	135	NHIL	178 l	JT
6 c	CC	51 t	CC	102 c	PB	140	CC	178 c	PG
6 r	CC	51 b	PG	102 r	OI	142 c	NC	178 r	JT
7 l	PA	52	CC	103	CC	142 r	DPPI	179 l	CC
7 c	PEP	57	NHIL/NC	105 tr	CC	143	NC	179 r	JT
7 r	DG	62	NHIL/MN	105 br	CC	150	DPPI	180 l	JT
8 r	OI	63	NHIL/MN	105 c	OI	149 r	NC	180 r	JT
13	CC	64 c	NHIL/MS	107 tl	CC	149 t	OI	181 l	NHIL/NC
17	OI	64 r	CC	107 tr	CC	149 b	RAY	181 r	JT
18 l	CC	65	CC	107 bl	OI	151 tl	DPPI	182	NHIL/NC
18 c	NHIL/NC	66 tl	NHIL/MS	107 br	Kos	152 l	NC	183 l	PG
18 r	CC	66 tc	NHIL/NC	108 l	PB	152 c	PG	183 r	PG
20 l	NHIL/MN	66 tr	NHIL/MS	108 r	Kos/CB	152 r	GI	184 l	CC
20 br	CC	66 bl & c	NHIL/MS	109 t	PB	153	OI	184 r	PG
20 tr	OI	66 br	NHIL/NC	109 b	CC	154 l	CC	185	NHIL/NC
21 l	PA	67	PG	112 l	CC	154 tr	PPL	186 l	PG
21 r	CC	68	NHIL/MS	112 c	NHIL/NA	154 br	SIL/PG	186 tr	JT
24 b	NC	71	SIL/PG	112 r	SIL/PG	155	NC	187 l	JT
24 t	NHIL/NC	73	CC	113	CC	156	DG	187 tr	JT
25	PG	77	CC	114 l	NHIL	157	NHIL/NC	187 br	JT
26	NHIL/NC	79 bl	TF	114 r	NHIL	158	PPL/JLJ		
29	TM	79 br	CC	116 l	NHIL/PG	159	CC	l =	left
30 l	CC	82 l	NHIL/MN	116 tr	NHll	160	CC	c =	centre
30 c	CC	82 c	KS	116 br	NHIL	161	Kos/HT	r =	right
30 r	PG	82 r	HH/PC	117	Ray	162 l	CC	t =	top
31 l	PG	83	OI	119	OI	162 c	PhotoB/PB	b =	bottom
31 r	CC	84 t	NA	120	DPPI	162 r	PPL/DS		
33	CC	84 c	SIL/PG	121	NHIL	163	TM		
34 l	CC	84 t	NA	122	NHIL/NC	164	PPL/BP		
34 r	NHIL/MN	85 t	NA	123	NHIL	165 tl	CC		
35 l	PG	85 b	CC	124	OI	165 bl & r	NHIL/NC		
35 tr	PG	86 t	NHIL/NA	125	NHIL	166	NHIL/NC		
36 t	NHIL/NC	86 b	NHIL/NC	126	NHIL	167	NC		

CC – Christel Clear; DG – Dale Granger; DPPI – DPPI; GI – Getty Images; HH/PC – Hedgehog House (Peter Cleary); Inpra – Inpra; JT – Jeff Toghill; Kos – Kos; Kos/BG – Kos (Bob Grieser); Kos/CB – Kos (Carlo Borlenghi); Kos/HT – Kos (Henri Thibault); Kos/GM-R – Kos (Gilles Martin-Roget); KS – K. Soehata; NA – Nick Aldridge; NC – Neil Corder; NHIL – New Holland Image Library; NHIL/MN – New Holland Image Library (Michael Ng); NHIL/MS – New Holland Image Library (Maryann Shaw); NHIL/NC – New Holland Image Library (Neil Corder); OI – Ocean Images; OvdW – Onne van der Wal; PA – Photo Access; PB – Picture Box; PEP – Patrick Eden Photography; PG – Peter Goldman; PhotoB/PB – Photo Bank (Peter Baker); PPL/AM – PPL (Adrian Morgan); PPL/BP – PPL (Barry Pickthall); PPL/DS – PPL (Dave Smyth); PPL/JLJ – PPL (Jamie Lawson-Johnson); Ray – Raymarine Ltd; RHPL – Robert Harding Picture Library; SIL – Struik Image Library; SIL/PG – Struik Image Library (Peter Goldman); TF – Terry Fong; TI/AH – Travel Ink (Angela Hampton); TL – Touchline; TM – The Moorings.

Illustrations by Robert Last, Stephen Felmore and Dennis Bagnall.
World map on p139 produced using Mountain High Maps © Digital Wisdom.
Charts supplied by the UK Hydrographic Office, except those on pp 133 (c) and 114 (r); SA Navy Hydrographic Office.